BIBLE SUDOKU

Published by Christian Art Publishers
PO Box 1599, Vereeniging, 1930, RSA

First edition 2023

Designed by Christian Art Publishers

Cover designed by Christian Art Publishers

Images used under license from Shutterstock.com

Printed in China

ISBN 978-0-638-00036-8

23 24 25 26 27 28 29 30 31 32 – 10 9 8 7 6 5 4 3 2 1

BIBLE SUDOKU

100 SUDOKU PUZZLES

FROM BEGINNER TO MASTER

INTRODUCTION

Did you know that playing sudoku ...

- boosts logical thinking?
- improves memory and recall?
- helps to develop quick-thinking skills?
- helps to improve concentration?
- minimizes the negative impact of dementia?
- helps to reduce anxiety and stress?
- is a great way to develop problem-solving skills?
- is a healthy form of escapism?
- is known to reduce overthinking?
- teaches resourcefulness?

Apart from all the health benefits, ***Bible Sudoku*** is designed to introduce you to the world of sudoku and provide you with a variety of puzzles to test your skills. The 100 puzzles with five degrees of difficulty, make it perfect for players of all skill levels.

Playing ***Bible Sudoku*** as a family can also be a great bonding experience. It allows family members to work together to solve puzzles and provides an opportunity for friendly competition. It can also be a great way to teach children some facts about the Bible as clues from the Bible make it easy for beginners to solve puzzles.

Bible Sudoku is a fun and entertaining puzzle game that the whole family can enjoy. So, gather the family and get ready for some fun and challenging puzzle-solving.

FOR BEGINNERS

Complete each grid
so that every row and column,
as well as every square,
contains the numbers 1 to 9.
No number can be repeated or left out.
Use the clues if you need help.

Challenge 1

	1	2	3	4	5	6	7	8	9
A		2	7	9		4	3		
B		3	5	6		1	8	4	
C	6		8		7	3		2	1
D			1	3				7	6
E		7	2		6	8		9	4
F	5	9		2	4				3
G	2	1	9	7	3	6		5	
H	8			4		5		1	2
I		5		8	1			3	9

A1, E4, F7
How many goats did Aaron sacrifice to the Lord on the Day of Atonement? (Lev. 16:9)

A5, D2, F8, G9
How many sons did Jesse, David's father, have? (1 Sam. 16:10-12)

A8, F3, H2, I7
How far along in her pregnancy was Elizabeth when Mary went to visit her? (Luke 1:36)

A9, C4, D5, E7
How many sheep did Nabal's wife, Abigail, give to David and his men? (1 Sam. 25:18-20)

B1, C7, D6, H5
What number was the plague of complete darkness? (Exod. 10:21)

B5, D7, I6
How many testaments are in the Bible?

B9, F6, H7, I1
How many demons did Jesus drive out of Mary Magdalene? (Luke 8:2)

C2, D1, G7, I3
How many Gospels are there in the New Testament?

E1, H3
In how many divine Persons does God exist? (1 John 5:7-8)

1, 8, 6, 5, 9, 2, 7, 4, 3

BEGINNER

Challenge 2

	1	2	3	4	5	6	7	8	9
A		2	7			1		3	
B	1			9			6	5	2
C		5	6	4	8				1
D	5	6				3	4		
E	8		9				1	6	
F		1	3		7			9	
G		4	5	3		8		2	9
H	7		8	2		9			
I	2			7	6	5		4	8

A1, C7, D5, I2
How many sons were born to David in Jerusalem whose mother was not Bathsheba, the daughter of Ammiel? (1 Chron. 3:5-8)

A4, F6, G1, H9
How many months is John the Baptist older than Jesus? (Luke 1:36)

A5, E4, F9, H7
What number was the plague against livestock? (Exod. 9:1-3)

A7, B2, D8, F4
In the parable of the talents, how many talents did the man entrust to his servants in total? (Matt. 25:15)

A9, B3, E6, F1, H5
How many sons, apart from Jesus, did Mary have? (Mark 6:3)

B5, C1, E9, H2, I7
How many decks were there in Noah's ark? (Gen. 6:16)

B6, C8, D9, E2, G7
How many seals were on the scroll in John's vision of heaven? (Rev. 5:1)

C6, D3, E5, F7
How many people lived in the Garden of Eden? (Gen. 2)

D4, G5, H8, I3
How many times did Joseph and Mary have to flee with baby Jesus? (Matt. 2:14-21)

9, 6, 5, 8, 4, 3, 7, 2, 1

Challenge 3

	1	2	3	4	5	6	7	8	9
A	9		6		7	5	1	3	
B		5		1		4	9		
C		7					2		
D		3		6	8				
E	6						5	9	
F		1		3		2	4	8	
G			3					7	
H		2		8					4
I			4			1			

A2, C8, D1, E4, G5
On which day did God create the sun, moon and stars? (Gen. 1:14-19)

A4, B1, D8, E3, G9, I5
How many letters did Paul write to the Thessalonians?

A9, B3, C6, E2, G7, I1
What number was the plague of locusts? (Exod. 10:1-4)

B5, C1, E9, H6, I7
How many times did Jesus leave His sleeping disciples to pray in the Garden of Gethsemane? (Matt. 26:39-44)

B8, C5, F9, G6, H7, I2
What number was the plague of boils? (Exod. 9:8-9)

B9, D7, E6, F1, H3, I4
How many churches in Asia did John write a letter to in Revelation? (Rev. 1:4)

C3, D9, E5, G1, H8
How many chapters are in the Old Testament book Obadiah?

C4, D6, F3, G2, H5, I9
How many sons did Shem have? (1 Chron. 1:17)

C9, D3, F5, G4, H1, I8
How many books in the Bible did Moses write? (Hint: He wrote the books from Genesis to Deuteronomy)

4, 2, 8, 3, 6, 7, 1, 9, 5

Challenge 4

	1	2	3	4	5	6	7	8	9
A				5				3	2
B	3		8			1		7	4
C	2	9	6	3	4	7		5	
D	8	6		2	1	4			
E	9	3			7	5		6	
F	1		7	6	3	9	8		
G	6	1		4	9	2		8	7
H		4	2			8		1	
I			9		5			2	

A1, E3, F8, I7
How many books in the New Testament only have one chapter?

A2, D7, H4, I1
How many times did Naaman have to bathe in the Jordan River to cure his leprosy? (2 Kings 5:10)

A3, C7, E9, I4
How many daughters did Leah have? (Gen. 34:1)

A5, C9, E4, I2
How many years had Aeneas been bedridden when Peter found him? (Acts 9:33)

A6, B7, H5, I9
During the war at Gath, there was a huge man who fought against the Philistines. How many fingers did he have on each hand? (2 Sam. 21:20)

A7, B4, D8, H9
Which of the Ten Commandments says that you shall not give false testimony? (Exod. 20:1-17)

B2, D3, F9, H1
On what day did God create the fish and birds? (Gen. 1:20-23)

B5, E7, F2
On what day did God create the sky? (Gen. 1:8)

D9, G3, H7, I6
After the Israelites left the Red Sea, how many days did they travel without water? (Exod. 15:22-23)

4, 7, 1, 8, 6, 9, 5, 2, 3

Challenge 5

	1	2	3	4	5	6	7	8	9
A	4	6	2	3			7	9	1
B	5	8	7	9	1	2		3	
C		9		4		7		5	2
D	2			8			6		
E			4		2	6	3		
F	8	5		7	3			1	
G	3	2	8	5		1	9	6	4
H	6				8		1	7	3
I		1	9		4		5		

A5, D6, E9, H3
How many tables did Solomon have made for the temple that had to be placed on the south side of the main room? (2 Chron. 4:8)

A6, C7, E8, I9
How many days after a baby boy's birth was Abraham told to circumcise him? (Gen. 17:12)

B7, D8, F6, H2
How many days had Lazarus been dead when Jesus brought him back to life? (John 11:39)

B9, C5, F3, I4
How many sons did Leah have? (Gen. 30:20)

C1, D3, E4
How many ribs did God take from Adam to make Eve? (Gen. 2:21)

C3, D2, I6
How many Christian virtues are named in 1 Corinthians 13:13?

D5, E1, F9, H6
How many blessings are recounted in the Beatitudes? (Matt. 5:3-11)

D9, E2, G5, I1
How many years of famine in Egypt did Joseph predict? (Gen. 41:30)

F7, H4, I8
How many disciples were named James? (Matt. 10:2-3)

5, 8, 4, 6, 1, 3, 9, 7, 2

Challenge 6

	1	2	3	4	5	6	7	8	9
A		8				1	3	6	7
B			7		8	3	9	5	
C		6			4		2		
D	6			8	1	4		2	
E	2			3		6	7	4	1
F		5		2	7	9		8	3
G		4	5	1	3	2		9	
H	9		2			8	1		5
I		1	6	5	9	7	4	3	

A1, C6, D7, E5
How many books of the law are there in the Bible?

A3, B9, F1, H4
How many people did King Nebuchadnezzar see walking around unharmed in the fiery furnace? (Dan. 3:25)

A4, C3, D9, E2
How many disciples did Jesus have? Now subtract 3 from that amount. What amount do you get? (Matt. 10:1-4)

A5, B2, I9
How many people from the Old Testament appeared at the transfiguration of Jesus? (Matt. 17:3)

B1, C8, F3
How many daughters did David have? (1 Chron. 3:9)

B4, F7, G9, H5
On what day did God create man? (Gen. 1:27-31)

C1, D3, H2
How many sons did Noah have? (Gen. 6:10)

C4, D2, G1, H8
Over how many days was the Festival of Unleavened Bread celebrated? (Exod. 12:14-17)

C9, E3, G7, I1
Adam lived another ______ hundred years after Seth was born. (Gen. 5:4)

5, 4, 9, 2, 1, 6, 3, 7, 8

Challenge 7

	1	2	3	4	5	6	7	8	9
A		1		4	2	9			
B	3	8	2			1	9		6
C	7	4			6	3		5	1
D	4	9	8	6		7	5		
E	1				9	2		8	7
F	2	5		3	8	4	6		
G			5	1					3
H	6	7	1	9	3			2	4
I		3		2	7	8			5

A1, B5, E4, H6
How many Amorite kings joined forces to attack Gibeon? (Josh. 10:5)

A3, E2, G6, I8
How many days were Joshua's men told to march around the city of Jericho? (Josh. 6:3)

A7, D8, E3
How many disciples did Jesus take with Him to the mountain where He was transfigured? (Matt. 17:1-2)

A8, B4, F3, G7
What number was the plague that brought hailstones? (Exod. 9:13-35)

A9, C4, G1, H7
How many tables were there in the room used to prepare animal sacrifices? (Ezek. 40:41)

B8, E7, G5, I3
How many books in the Bible are named after John?

C3, F9, G8, I1
How many years did King Hoshea reign over Israel? (2 Kings 17:1)

C7, D9, G2
How many men in the Bible never experienced physical death? (Gen. 5:22-24; 2 Kings 2:11)

D5, F8, I7
What verse in Psalm 23 starts with the words "The Lord is my Shepherd"?

5, 6, 3, 7, 8, 4, 9, 2, 1

BEGINNER

Challenge 8

	1	2	3	4	5	6	7	8	9
A	6	3	8		1	2		5	
B	7	1	4		8			2	3
C	5		9	6			1		8
D	1	7		5	9		8	3	
E	4	6	5		7		2		
F			3	4					
G	9		6		3	4	7	1	2
H			1	2	5	7	9		6
I	2	4				9	3	8	

A4, C8, F9, I3
How many years did it take Solomon to build the temple? (1 Kings 6:38)

A7, C5, D9, H8
How many beasts did Daniel see in his vision? (Dan. 7:4-7)

A9, B4, E8, F2
How many of the lepers whom Jesus healed did not turn back to thank Him? (Luke 17:12-17)

B6, F7, G2, I9
How old was Mephibosheth when he learned that his father, Jonathan, was dead? (2 Sam. 4:4)

B7, D6, F8, I5
How many days of the week were Israelites permitted to work? (Exod. 20:9)

C2, D3, F5
How many sons did the father in the parable of the lost son have? (Luke 15:11)

C6, E4, H1
In how many different languages was this notice above the cross written: "Jesus of Nazareth, King of the Jews"? (John 19:19-20)

E6, F1, G4, H2
In what chapter of Revelation are the seven trumpets first mentioned?

E9, F6, I4
In the parable of the lost sheep, how many sheep did the shepherd have to look for?

7, 4, 9, 5, 6, 2, 3, 8, 1

Challenge 9

	1	2	3	4	5	6	7	8	9
A			9		1		2	8	4
B		2		7	9		3		5
C	3		1		2	5		7	6
D	8	4	5	1	3	2	6	9	
E	9				6	4	5	3	2
F				5	7		8	4	1
G	1	7	3				4		
H	2	6	8			1	7		
I		9			8	7		6	3

A1, D9, E3
On what day did God rest after completing creation? (Gen. 2:1-3)

A2, G5, H8, I1
In what chapter of Acts do Ananias and Sapphira pay the price for lying to the Holy Spirit?

A4, B3, F1, G6
How many wings did each of the four living creatures in John's vision have? (Rev. 4:8)

A6, F2, H4
How many servants received talents in the parable of the talents? (Matt. 25:14-15)

B1, C4, H5, I3
How many men only ate vegetables and only drank water for ten days? (Dan. 1:11-12)

B6, C2, E4, G9
How many years was Abdon the leader of Israel? (Judges 12:13-14)

B8, E2, I7
How many chapters are there in the New Testament book of Philemon?

C7, F6, G4, H9
Twelve precious stones were used to decorate the foundations of the wall. Which foundation stone was decorated with topaz? (Rev. 21:19-20)

F3, G8, I4
How many wives did Jacob have? (Gen. 29:25-30)

7, 5, 6, 3, 4, 8, 1, 9, 2

BEGINNER

Challenge 10

	1	2	3	4	5	6	7	8	9
A	7	2		8	6	4	5		9
B			8	1	5				
C		6	9			3	4		8
D		9	7	3				2	4
E		4	6		9				
F	2	8	5			1			
G	9	7		5	1	6	3		2
H	8	1	3	4		7			5
I	6		2		3		1		7

A3, C8, D1, E9
How many scrolls are mentioned in Revelation 5:1?

A8, B2, E1, F9
How many days was Jonah in the belly of the whale? (Matt. 12:40)

B1, F5, G3, I8
How many faces and wings did each of the living creatures in the fire have? (Ezek. 1:4-6)

B6, F8, H7, I4
Which verse in 1 Chronicles 3:1-9 mentions David's daughter?

B7, C4, E6, H5
How many boats were filled up with fish after Jesus told them to let their nets down? (Luke 5:7)

B8, C5, E4, F7
How many braids of Samson's hair did Delilah cut off? (Judges 16:19)

B9, D7, F4, H8
How many days after Jesus had told His disciples what would happen to Him did He lead Peter, James and John up a very high mountain? (Matt. 17:1)

C1, D6, E8, I2
How many loaves of bread did Jesus multiply to feed 5,000 men? (Matt. 14:17)

D5, E7, G8, I6
How old was Josiah when he became king? (2 Chron. 34:1)

1, 3, 4, 9, 2, 7, 6, 5, 8

Challenge 11

	1	2	3	4	5	6	7	8	9
A			1			2	6	5	
B	2	3		5	4				9
C	8		7			6		4	2
D		6	5				9		4
E				7	5		8	3	
F	7		8		3	9	1	2	
G		7		4		3	5	8	1
H	9		3	1	2				7
I		1	4		6			9	

A1, E6, F2, H7
How many thousand stalls did Solomon have for his horses and chariots? (2 Chron. 9:25)

A2, C4, E3, G5
How many bulls were to be sacrificed on the fifth day of the Festival of Trumpets? (Num. 29:26)

A4, C7, D1, I9
How many daughters-in-law did Noah have? (Gen. 7.13)

A5, B7, D8, I6
How many female lambs did Abraham give to Abimelech to prove that he had dug the well called Beersheba? (Gen. 21:28-31)

A9, B6, D5, H2, I4
How many sons did Abraham's brother Nahor and his wife, Milcah, have? (Gen. 22:20-23)

B3, E9, F4, G1, H8
How many steps did the people carrying the Ark of the Lord take when David stopped to sacrifice an ox and a fattened calf? (2 Sam. 6:13)

B8, C5, D6, E1
How many sons did Esau have with his wife Adah? (Gen. 36:4)

C2, F9, H6, I1
How many curtains were to be sewn together according to Exodus 26:3?

D4, E2, G3, I7
How many great lights did God make? (Gen. 1:16)

2, 5, 1, 6, 8, 7, 3, 9, 4

BEGINNER

Challenge 12

	1	2	3	4	5	6	7	8	9
A	1		4		5	6		9	
B				7	1	3		5	2
C	2		3				7	6	
D		8	1					2	
E	5			6				7	
F		4		9	8	5	6		3
G	9	6		4			1	8	7
H	4	2			9			3	
I	3		7			8	2		

A2, D5, F1, H6
How many angels did John notice in Revelation 8:2?

A4, E5, F3, G6
How many chapters are in the Old Testament book Haggai?

A7, D4, E2, G5
How many crosses were there on Golgotha? (Mark 15:27)

A9, B1, C4, E7, H3
How many groups were Ithamar's descendants divided into? (1 Chron. 24:4)

B2, C6, D7, E3, I9
How many fruits of the Spirit are listed in Galatians 5:22-23?

B3, D1, H9, I5
How long did it take God to create the heavens and the earth, the sea, and all that is in them? (Exod. 20:11)

B7, C5, D6, E9, I8
How many horns were they instructed to make for the altar of burnt offering? (Exod. 27:1-2)

C2, D9, G3, H7, I4
How many kings are listed in Genesis 14:2?

C9, E6, F8, H4, I2
How many different languages did the people speak when they first started building the Tower of Babel? (Gen. 11:1)

7, 2, 3, 8, 9, 6, 4, 5, 1

Challenge 13

	1	2	3	4	5	6	7	8	9
A	5		9	2		6		1	4
B			6	4			8		
C	7				3			5	9
D	1		7	9		4	2	8	3
E			2	5				7	
F	8		3	1		7			
G	2					9		6	
H	4		5		1	2		3	8
I		6	1	3		8	7		

A2, C4, E5, G3
How long were the Israelites forced to serve Cushan-Rishathaim, king of Mesopotamia? (Judges 3:8)

A5, B9, G4, H2
How old was Joash when he became king? (2 Chron. 24:1)

A7, B1, E6, G2
How many days had the masses already spent with Jesus before He fed them? (Mark 8:2)

B2, C6, E9, G7
How many members of Saul's family were still alive when David asked after them? (2 Sam. 9:1-3)

B5, E2, F8, H7, I1
How many kings were involved in the first war mentioned in the Bible? (Gen. 14:1-2)

B6, D2, F7, G9, I5
How many women appear in the book of the genealogy of Jesus Christ? (Matt. 1:1-16)

B8, C2, F5, I9
How many sons did Judah and Tamar have? (Matt. 1:3)

C3, E7, F2, G5, I8
Into how many riverheads did the main river flowing out of Eden separate? (Gen. 2:10)

C7, D5, E1, F9, H4
How many of the Lord's followers went with Peter that day? (Acts 11:11-12)

8, 7, 3, 1, 9, 5, 2, 4, 6

Challenge 14

BEGINNER

	1	2	3	4	5	6	7	8	9
A		7		3	6				
B		4			1	5		2	6
C		2	5	8		4	3	1	9
D	7	6			2	1	9		
E		9		5				8	1
F			1		9			4	7
G	4	3			8			9	2
H	5		6	2	4				3
I				7	5	3	8		

A1, G4, H7, I2
How many things does David ask of God in Psalm 27:4?

A3, B4, H6, I1
How many kings were involved in the first war mentioned in the Bible? (Gen. 14:1-2)

A6, E1, F7, I3
How many daughters did Saul have? (1 Sam. 14:49)

A7, D4, E3, I9
How many chapters are there in the New Testament book Philippians?

A8, D9, F2, G7
How many Amorite kings went into battle against Gibeon? (Josh. 10:5)

A9, B1, D3, F6, H2
Which of the ten commandments says you shall not steal? (Exod. 20:1-17)

B3, D8, E5, F1
How many chapters are there in the Old Testament book Nahum?

B7, C5, E6, G3, H8
Every how many years is considered a Sabbath rest? (Lev. 25:4)

C1, E7, F4, G6, I8
How many years did Jephthah serve Israel as a judge? (Judges 12:7)

1, 9, 2, 4, 5, 8, 3, 7, 6

Challenge 15

	1	2	3	4	5	6	7	8	9
A								1	8
B	9			3					4
C	2		8	5		4	9	6	
D	7			1		3			5
E		8	6		4	2		3	
F	4		1	7			6	9	
G	8	2	7			6	3	5	
H	6		9		3			7	1
I	1	5		2		7		8	

A1, C9, F2, I3
How many chapters are there in the Old Testament book Joel?

A2, B7, C5, E9
How many times will the person who kills Cain be punished? (Gen. 4:15)

A3, D8, G4, H2, I7
Esau had ______ hundred men with him when he met Jacob. (Gen. 33:1)

A4, B2, D5, I9
How many days before the Passover did Jesus arrive in Bethany? (John 12:1)

A5, B8, D3, F9, H7
A person alone can be overpowered, but ______ can defend themselves. (Eccles. 4:12)

A6, D2, E4, G9, I5
How many years, minus 20, did Hezekiah reign as king? (2 Kings 18:1-2)

A7, B3, E1, F5, H6
How many of his brothers did Joseph introduce to Pharaoh? (Gen. 47:2)

B5, D7, F6, H4
How many verses are in Psalm 101?

B6, C2, E7, G5
How many chapters are in the New Testament book Second John?

3, 7, 4, 6, 2, 9, 5, 8, 1

BEGINNER

Challenge 16

	1	2	3	4	5	6	7	8	9
A			6	8		5			3
B	1		4			2		8	6
C			8	4		7	9	1	5
D	5	2		6		8	1		
E	4		9		7		3		2
F		1	7		3		8		4
G		4		9	5	6	2		7
H		9		1	2	3	6		
I	3			7		4	5	9	

A1, B5, D9, F6,
How many bulls had to be sacrificed on the fifth day of the Feast of Tabernacles? (Num. 29:26)

A2, B7, D8, H1
How many brothers did David have? (1 Sam. 16:10-12)

A5, E6, G3, I9
Joseph interpreted the dreams of two men while in prison. Of those men, how many were set free? (Gen. 40:1-23)

A7, D5, H8
How many chapters does the Old Testament book Malachi have?

A8, C1, F4, I3
How many daughters did Lot have? (Gen. 19:16)

B2, E4, F8, H3
How many young women did not have enough oil in their lamps? (Matt. 25:1-13)

B4, C2, D3, G8
How many times did Peter betray Jesus? (Mark 14:66-72)

C5, E8, F1, I2
How many years did Jehosheba keep Joash hidden in the temple? (2 Kings 11:1-3)

E2, G1, H9, I5
How many oxen did Moses give to the Merarites for their work? (Num. 7:8)

9, 7, 1, 4, 2, 5, 3, 6, 8

Challenge 17

	1	2	3	4	5	6	7	8	9
A	4	5		6	1		8		3
B	1	8		9	5		4	2	
C			2		7	8		6	5
D		7	9		3		5		4
E	3		1	8		5	6		
F	5	6			2				1
G	7	9	5	3	8				6
H		2		5	4	9	7	1	
I			4	2		7		5	

A3, B9, E8, F4
There are 6 things the Lord hates, but how many does He detest? (Prov. 6:16)

A6, D1, E9, G7
Before the rooster crows ______, Peter would deny Jesus three times. (Mark 14:72)

A8, C1, E5, F7, I9
It took Joab and his men ______ months and 20 days to finish the census. (2 Sam. 24:2, 8)

B3, D6, H1, I5
How many stone water jars did Jesus turn into wine at the wedding in Cana? (John 2:6)

B6, C2, F8, H3, I7
How many gates were on each side of the wall? (Rev. 21:13)

C4, E2, F6, G8
How many living creatures did John see? (Rev. 4:6)

C7, D4, G6, I2
There is ______ Lord ______ faith, ______ baptism. (Eph. 4:5-6)

D8, F3, H9, I1
Adam lived ______ hundred years after Seth was born. (Gen. 5:4)

7, 2, 9, 6, 3, 4, 1, 8

BEGINNER

Challenge 18

	1	2	3	4	5	6	7	8	9
A	6			1	9				3
B	5	9		7				6	2
C	2		3	5		8	4	7	
D		8		2	4	5			6
E	3	7		9	8		2		
F	4				7	3	8		1
G	7		5		1		9		
H	9		4	3			6	1	8
I		6	1	4	2			5	

A2, B6, E8, G9
How many unmarried daughters did Philip have? (Acts 21:8-9)

A3, D7, H6, I9
How many days did Paul and the others stay with the disciples in Tyre? (Acts 21:3-4)

A6, F3, G8, H2
How many angels saved Lot and his family from Sodom? (Gen. 19:1)

A7, E9, F2, H5
The locusts were told to torment the people who did not have the seal of God for ______ months. (Rev. 9:1-5)

A8, B3, G4, I1
How many days, divided by 5, was Jesus tempted by the devil? (Matt. 4:1-2)

B7, C2, D1, E6
How many soldiers pierced Jesus' side with a spear? (John 19:34)

B5, D8, G2, I7
How many months did Moses' mother hide him? (Heb. 11:23)

C5, E3, F4, G6
Paul stayed in Corinth for 1 year and ______ months teaching the Word of God. (Acts 18:7-11)

C9, D3, F8, I6
How many chapters are in the Old Testament book Amos?

4, 7, 2, 5, 8, 1, 3, 6, 9

Challenge 19

	1	2	3	4	5	6	7	8	9
A		1		5	9	3	2		
B	9		6		1	7		4	
C	3		8	6			7		1
D		9	1	2		5	8	7	4
E	2		4		8	9	1	5	
F		7		1				3	2
G	5	6				8	3	1	
H		4		3	2	1			5
I	1	8		9		6	4		7

A1, C5, F6, G4
How many chapters are in the Old Testament book Jonah?

A3, E4, G5, H1
How many plagues did the seven angels bring? (Rev. 15:1)

A8, D1, E9, F5, H7
On the day of the New Moon, 1 young bull, ______ lambs and 1 ram, all without defect, were to be sacrificed. (Ezek. 46:6)

A9, B4, F1, H8
How many people were on Noah's ark? (Gen. 7:13)

B2, C6, G3, I8
How many daughters did Laban have? (Gen. 29:16)

B7, C2, F3, I5
How many times did Paul receive the 40 lashes, minus one, from the Jews? (2 Cor. 11:24)

B9, D5, E2, I3
After ______ years, Paul went up to Jerusalem to see Peter. (Gal. 1:18)

C8, F7, G9, H3
On day ______, Abidan brought his offering. (Num. 7:60)

4, 7, 6, 8, 2, 5, 3, 9

Challenge 20

	1	2	3	4	5	6	7	8	9
A		2	8	9		6		5	3
B		3	9		5	8			
C			4		1		8		6
D	7			2		4	9		
E	3			1		5	6	7	4
F	4		5	7					1
G	9	1	3		4		5		2
H	2			6	9	1	3		8
I			6		2		7		

A1, B7, D3, I8
How many sons did Abigail have? (1 Chron. 2:17)

A5, B9, C2, G6, H3
How many chapters are in the Old Testament book Micah?

A7, B4, H8, I2
How many friends carried the paralyzed man to Jesus? (Mark 2:3)

B1, D2, F5, G8
Noah was ______ hundred years old when God flooded the earth. (Gen. 7:6, 11)

B8, C6, E3, F7
There are ______ unchangeable things in which it is impossible for God to lie. (Heb. 6:18)

C1, D9, H2, I4
The 10 Commandments halved.

C4, D5, F8, I6
How many times did Paul beg the Lord to remove the thorn from his side? (2 Cor. 12:8)

C8, E2, F6, I9
In which of the first 10 chapters of Genesis, verse 14, does the rainbow appear in the sky?

D8, E5, F2, G4, I1
How many verses does Psalm 130 have?

1, 7, 4, 6, 2, 5, 3, 9, 8

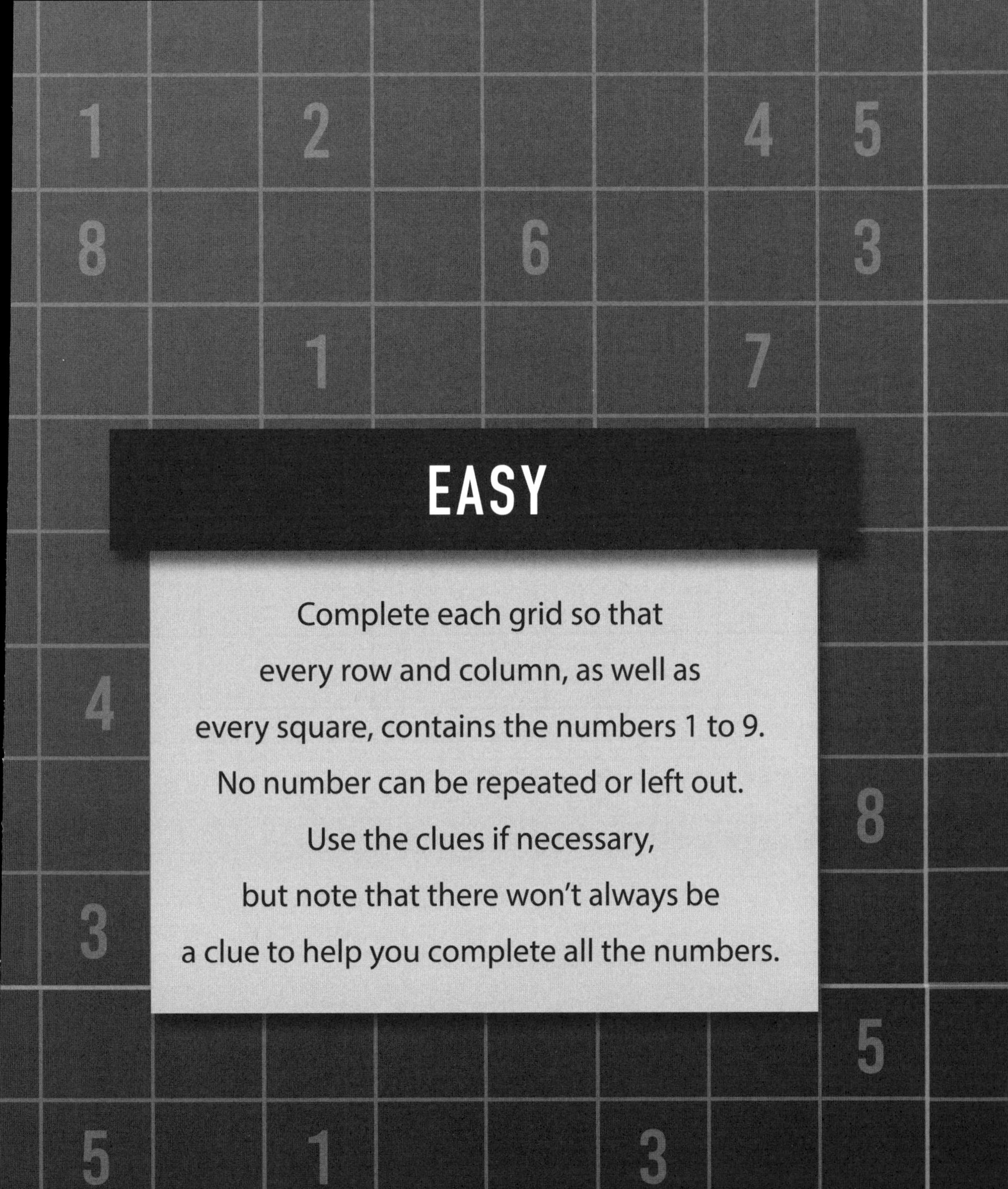

EASY

Complete each grid so that every row and column, as well as every square, contains the numbers 1 to 9. No number can be repeated or left out. Use the clues if necessary, but note that there won't always be a clue to help you complete all the numbers.

Challenge 21

	1	2	3	4	5	6	7	8	9
A	9		1	8	2		6		
B	6			9				7	
C	8			3	5				
D			6			8			
E		5		4		9	7	6	3
F			9	2			1		
G	4						9		1
H			7						
I								2	

A2, F6, H5, I3
How many sons did Esau and Oholibamah have? (Gen. 36:5)

A8, D4, G6, H1, I7
_____ times Paul received the 40 lashes, minus one, from the Jews. (2 Cor. 11:24)

A9, C3, F2, H8, I6
Into how many riverheads did the main river which flowed out of Eden separate? (Gen. 2:10)

B6, C8, D2, H4
How many sons did Ruth and Boaz have? (Ruth 4:13)

C2, D5, G4, I9
How many sons did Jesse have besides David? (1 Sam. 17:12)

C6, F5, I4
The Lord blessed Job with _____ thousand camels. (Job 42:12)

C9, D8
How many gifts of the Spirit are there according to 1 Corinthians 12:8-10?

D9, E1, G3
On which day did God separate the waters from the sky? (Gen. 1:6-8)

E3, H7, I2
Josiah was _____ years old when he became king. (2 Chron. 34:1)

1 = E5, I1; 2 = B2, C7, H6; 3 = B7, D1, G8; 4 = B5, D7; 5 = B3, F9; 6 = G2, H9; 7 = A6, F1; 8 = B9, F8, G5; 9 = H2, I5

3, 5, 4, 1, 7, 6, 9, 2, 8

Challenge 22

	1	2	3	4	5	6	7	8	9
A		8	7		1				4
B				3				1	
C	6						2		
D		6		7					
E		2		6					
F			1			5		4	7
G		4	8	1					6
H	2				9		1	3	
I		9				8			5

EASY

A4, D8, E6, F1
Psalm 149 has ______ verses (amount).

A8, F7, I5
On what day did God create man? (Gen. 1:27-31)

B2, D3, E8, H4
Psalm 100 has ______ verses (amount).

B3, G8, I4
How many rams were to be sacrificed on the fifth day? (Num. 29:26)

B5, D1, F4
How many years did Jehoram rule in Jerusalem? (2 Kings 8:17)

C4, E3, H6
How many gold rings were cast and placed on the Ark? (Exod. 37:3)

C6, H2, I8
If you add up all the chapters in First, Second and Third John, how many chapters are there altogether?

C9, F2, G6, I3
How many friends tried to comfort Job? (Job 2:11)

D6, E9
How many pairs of every kind of unclean animal were they instructed to take on the ark? (Gen. 7:2)

9, 6, 5, 2, 8, 4, 7, 3, 1

1 = C2, I1; 2 = A6, D9, F5; 3 = A1, D7, E5; 4 = B1, D5, I7; 5 = A7, C5, G1; 6 = B6, H3; 7 = B7, E1, G5; 8 = C8, E7, H9; 9 = B9, C3, G7

Challenge 23

	1	2	3	4	5	6	7	8	9
A		4						9	
B		1						7	3
C						6			
D	3		8			5	1		7
E					8	2	4		
F			4		1				
G			6		4				5
H				5		3		8	6
I	8		2			1	7		

A1, F4, H2
How many pairs of every kind of clean animal were they instructed to take on the ark? (Gen. 7:2)

A3, E8, F1
How many chapters are there in the Old Testament book Lamentations?

A4, E1, G8
How many times per day did the Israelites have to march around the city of Jericho? (Josh. 6:3)

A7, D5, I4
Psalm 128 has ______ verses (amount).

A9, C1, F2, H5
How many criminals were crucified on the same day as Jesus? (Mark 15:27)

B6, H1, I9
How many winds of heaven were stirring up the sea in Daniel's vision? (Dan. 7:2)

B7, F9, G4
If you add up all the chapters in First and Second Peter, how many chapters are there altogether?

C4, D2, E9, H7
Take the amount of days Jonah spent in the belly of the fish and multiply it by 3. (Jonah 1:17)

E4, F7, G2
How many times was Paul shipwrecked? (2 Cor. 11:25)

9 = B3, F6, G1, I5

1 = C9, H3; 2 = B4, D8, G7; 3 = A5, C3, I8; 4 = C8, D4; 5 = B5, C7, I2; 6 = B1, E2, F8; 7 = C5, E3, G6; 8 = A6, C2;

7, 5, 1, 6, 2, 4, 8, 9, 3

Challenge 24

	1	2	3	4	5	6	7	8	9
A						2			
B			4	3		5		1	8
C							2	5	
D	7	1	6			4			
E			3		7			9	
F			2				6		
G	9		5						6
H						3			
I	4		7		8				

EASY

A2, F1, I9
After ______ days the high priest Ananias, along with some elders and Tertullus, came to make their case against Paul. (Acts 24:1)

A4, E1, H3
If you added up the chapters in the Old Testament books Jonah and Malachi, how many chapters would you have altogether?

A7, E2, H4
How many anchors did the sailors drop because they were afraid that the ship might hit some rocks? (Acts 27:29)

B2, F8, H7
How many years extra did Jacob have to work for Laban to marry Rachel? (Gen. 29:25-27)

B5, C1, H2
Divide the number of Jesus' disciples by 2. (Matt. 10:1)

B7, C4, D5, I6
How many towns did the descendants of Aaron receive from the tribes Judah and Simeon? (Josh. 21:13-16)

C3, E9, G6, I7
They crucified other criminals alongside Jesus. ______ on His left and ______ on His right. (Mark 15:27)

C9, D7, F5
How many weeks did Daniel mourn? (Dan. 10:2)

E4, H8, I2
How many horns did the second beast that John saw coming out of the earth have? (Rev. 13:11)

8 = C2, D8, F6, G7; 9 = A3, F2, H9

1 = A5, F4, H1; 2 = B1, D9, G5; 3 = A1, G2, I8; 4 = C5, F9, G8; 5 = D4, E7, H5; 6 = A8, E6, I4; 7 = A9, C6, G4;

5, 8, 4, 7, 6, 9, 1, 3, 2

Challenge 25

	1	2	3	4	5	6	7	8	9
A	1	5						6	7
B									
C	4		3				5	1	
D	2	1		8					
E	8				7				
F			4			9	3		2
G		2	6		4			9	
H				3				7	
I			8	5					

A3, E6, I8
How many rooms did the tabernacle have? (Heb. 9:2-4)

A4, C9, H2, I5
Which verse in Luke 9 does Herod admit to beheading John?

A7, D6, I2
How many rows of precious stones were to be set in the breastplate? (Exod. 28:15-17)

B2, D9, F1, I6
Omri reigned in Tirzah for ______ years. (1 Kings 16:23)

B5, E9, H3
Paul spent ______ night and day in the open sea. (2 Cor. 11:25)

B6, E3, G9
Benjamin's portion was ______ times as much as anyone else's. (Gen. 43:34)

B8, D5, G1
How many branches did the chief cupbearer see on the vine in his dream? (Gen. 40:9-10)

C2, G7, H6
In which chapter of John is the woman who got caught in the act of adultery mentioned?

D7, F2, G4
How many times did Jacob bow before his brother, Esau? (Gen. 33:3)

2, 9, 4, 6, 1, 5, 3, 8, 7

1 = F4, G6, I7; 2 = B7, C4, H5; 3 = A6, E2, I9; 4 = B4, E8, H9; 5 = D8, F5, H1; 6 = C5, E4, H7; 7 = B3, C6, I1; 8 = A5, B9, F8;
9 = B1, D3, E7

Challenge 26

	1	2	3	4	5	6	7	8	9
A			9	6	4	7		2	
B					1		3		
C	8								7
D			4						5
E	5	3				2			
F		9						3	
G	7	6			8			9	
H		1						8	
I			2						

EASY

A2, C6, F5, G7
How many sparrows could you buy for two pennies? (Luke 12:6)

A9, D6, E7
Multiply the number of chapters in Malachi by 2.

B2, F9, G4
How many small copper coins did the poor widow give as an offering? (Mark 12:41-44)

C2, E8, F4, I7
How many chapters are in the Old Testament book Ruth?

C3, F1, G9
How many Mediators are needed to reconcile God with man? (1 Tim. 2:5)

C4, H6, I9
Which chapter in Ecclesiastes says that there is a time or a season for everything?

C7, D4, I1
How many sons did David have who were not born in Hebron or Jerusalem? (1 Chron. 3:1-9)

C8, F6, I5
The Israelites were instructed to march around the city of Jericho once every day for ______ days. (Josh. 6:3)

D2, E5, I8
Divide the number of chapters in the Old Testament book Hosea by 2.

5, 8, 2, 4, 1, 3, 9, 6, 7

1 = A7, D8, I6; 2 = C5, D1, H7; 3 = A1, D5, G3; 4 = B9, G6, H1; 5 = B8, H3, I4; 6 = B1, D7, E3, H9; 7 = B3, F7, H4; 8 = B4, F3, I2;
9 = B6, E9, H5

Challenge 27

	1	2	3	4	5	6	7	8	9
A			8		9			3	7
B	4		5						
C	9			7			6		1
D	7				3		1		
E			4						
F	8	3				5			9
G	6				1				2
H				4					5
I	2								

A2, D6, E9, I4
The Lord instructed Moses to take two onyx stones and engrave the names of the sons of Israel on them. _____ names on one stone and the remaining _____ on the other. (Exod. 28:9-10)

A4, B8, D3, F7
If you added up the chapters in Obadiah and Jude, how many chapters would you have altogether?

A7, D8, G4
The altar was to be built _____ cubits long and _____ cubits wide. (Exod. 27:1)

B4, G6, H1
After _____ months, they sailed on a ship from Malta to Rome. (Acts 28:11)

B6, F4, I8
According to Ephesians 4:4-6, we are called to _____ hope, _____ faith and _____ baptism.

C6, E8, H2, I5
How many chapters are in the Old Testament book Song of Songs?

C8, F5, I7
Peter was put in prison and guarded by _____ squads of soldiers. (Acts 12:4-5)

D2, G8, H6
Seth was _____ hundred and twelve years old when he died. (Gen. 5:8)

E5, G3, H7
How many days before the flood came did God tell Noah to enter the ark? (Gen. 7:4)

9 = B7, E4, I3
1 = A1, E2, H3; 2 = C2, E6, H5; 3 = C3, E7, I9; 4 = A6, D9, G2; 5 = C5, E1, I2; 6 = B5, F3, H8; 7 = B2, F8, I6; 8 = B9, D4, G7;
6, 2, 5, 3, 1, 8, 4, 9, 7

Challenge 28

	1	2	3	4	5	6	7	8	9
A							9		7
B				4	3				
C				2	6			4	
D			5						9
E			3	8		5	6		
F	1	8					4		
G						2	3		
H		6				1			
I			9		8			7	

EASY

A1, E8, F5, I7
How many verses does Psalm 117 have?

A5, B8, H7, I1
Abraham asked God whether He would still destroy Sodom if there were ______ less than 50 righteous people. (Gen. 18:28)

A6, B1, G3
How many chapters are in First and Second Peter altogether?

B2, D7, E5, H4
How many healthy cows did Pharaoh see in his dream? (Gen. 41:2)

B3, D1, I4
How many branches were to extend from the sides of the lampstand? (Exod. 25:32)

C1, E2, H8
The Israelites were instructed to eat the produce they'd already harvested until the ______ year when they could start eating from the new crop. (Lev. 25:22)

B7, C3, E9, G8
How many sons did Eliezer have? (1 Chron. 23:17)

C9, D4, H1
The ______ commandment says, "You shall not take the name of the Lord your God in vain." (Exod. 20:7)

D6, G2, H5
How many tassels were to be sewn onto the garment? (Deut. 22:12)

2, 5, 8, 7, 6, 9, 1, 3, 4

1 = A4, D5, I2; 2 = B9, D2, H3; 3 = A2, F8, H3; 4 = A3, E1, I9; 5 = C2, F9, G4; 6 = A8, F6, G9; 7 = C6, F3, G1; 8 = C7, D8, H9;
9 = B6, F4, G5

Challenge 29

	1	2	3	4	5	6	7	8	9
A									
B						8	2	1	
C			9					8	
D			7				6		
E			1			9			7
F	8		2		6			5	
G		9		5		7		3	
H		2		4	3		1		
I	5		4						

A1, B5, D6, F2
How many groups did Abimelech divide his soldiers in to ambush Shechem? (Judges 9:34)

A3, C7, D9, F6
The New Testament book Titus has ______ chapters.

A5, D8, G9
On how many onyx stones were the names of the sons of Israel to be engraved? (Exod. 28:9)

A7, B3, E5
How many verses does the Lord's Prayer in Matthew 6 consist of?

A8, C5, I7
How many healthy heads of grain did Pharaoh see in his dream? (Gen. 41:5)

B1, C4, G3, I8
Moses was instructed to select ______ towns to be the Israelites' cities of refuge, to which a person who had accidentally killed someone could flee. (Num. 35:9-13)

B9, D1, H8
On what day did Abidan bring his offering? (Num. 7:60)

C2, D5, I4
The Israelites were instructed to offer ______ ram as a burnt offering. (Lev. 16:5)

D4, H3, I9
If you added up all the chapters in First and Second Thessalonians, how many chapters would there be altogether?

4, 3, 2, 5, 7, 6, 9, 1, 8

1 = A6, F9, G1; 2 = C1, E4, I6; 3 = B4, E1, I2; 4 = C9, E8, G7; 5 = C6, D2, H9; 6 = A9, E2, H6; 7 = B2, F4, H1; 8 = A2, E7, G5;
9 = A4, F7, I5

Challenge 30

EASY

	1	2	3	4	5	6	7	8	9
A			4		6	3		8	
B	9							6	
C		7			5	2			4
D	8				7		3		9
E									
F	1				8				2
G					1		5		
H									6
I	5	4			3			9	

A1, E5, H3, I4
Rahab was the ______ woman (ordinal number) to be named in the genealogy of Jesus. (Matt. 1:1-16)

A2, D3, E8
When Joseph reunited with his brothers, how many years of famine were there left? (Gen. 45:1-15)

A7, F3, G2
First Samuel is the ______ book (ordinal number) listed in the Old Testament.

B2, C7, D6, H8
The waters flooded the earth for ______ hundred and fifty days. (Gen. 7:24)

B4, F8, G1, I7
How many years of abundance did Joseph say there would be? (Gen. 41:29)

B6, G4, H2
If you added up all the chapters in Philippians and Colossians, how many chapters would there be altogether?

C8, F2, G9
How many days after Jacob fled did Laban come to hear of it? (Gen. 31:22)

D4, F7, I6
How many years did Jephthah serve as judge? (Judges 12:7)

E1, F4, G6
The ______ commandment (ordinal number) tells us to keep the Sabbath day holy. (Exod. 20:8-11)

2, 5, 9, 1, 7, 8, 3, 6, 4

1 = A4, E9, I3; 2 = B7, D2, G8; 3 = B3, E4, H1; 4 = B5, D8, H7; 5 = B9, F6, H4; 6 = C1, E2, G3; 7 = A9, E3, H6; 8 = C3, E7, I9;
9 = C4, E6, H5

Challenge 31

	1	2	3	4	5	6	7	8	9
A			3	9	6				
B									
C			5	4		8		2	
D		1				6	2		
E			7	5		1			4
F		8					7	6	
G			9			5			
H		2	8					1	
I					9		3		

A2, B6, G8, H5
How many daughters did the priest of Midian have? (Exod. 2:16)

A7, B4, I3
Jesus honored His followers in the same way that God honored Him so that they may become ______. (John 17:22)

A9, F1, I2
The ______ commandment (ordinal number) tells us to honor our father and mother. (Exod. 20:12)

B1, F3, I4
The ______ commandment (ordinal number) tells us that we cannot worship any other gods. (Exod. 20:3-6)

B2, F5, G7, H1
The concubine left him and went to her father's house in Bethlehem where she stayed for ______ months. (Judges 19:1-2)

B8, D9, F4, H6
How many baskets of bread did the chief baker have on his head in his dream? (Gen. 40:16)

B9, D5, I8
How many steps did the stairway have which led up to the gate of the temple? (Ezek. 40:37)

C2, D1, E8
Galatians is the ______ book (ordinal number) listed in the New Testament.

C7, G1, H4
How many descendants did Shekaniah have? (1 Chron. 3:22)

7, 1, 5, 2, 4, 3, 8, 9, 6

1 = C1, F9, G5; 2 = A6, E5, G9; 3 = C5, E1, G2; 4 = A8, D3, I6; 5 = B5, D8, H7; 6 = B3, E2, I9; 7 = C9, D4, I1; 8 = A1, E7, G4;
9 = B7, F6, H9

Challenge 32

	1	2	3	4	5	6	7	8	9
A				3	9			2	
B		4	3			1	5		
C			6		7			3	
D	8	2			6			7	
E				9	8				
F								4	
G			2	5	1			6	
H				7				9	
I			8						

EASY

A2, B8, G9
Ruth is the ______ book (ordinal number) listed in the Old Testament.

B1, F3, I2
What chapter in Luke talks about Jesus' transfiguration?

B4, F1, I6
The ______ commandment (ordinal number) tells us that we shall not murder. (Exod. 20:13)

B9, F6, G2
How many days were the Israelites to go without yeast? (Exod. 12:19)

C1, F9, H7
How many wives did Jehoiada choose for Joash? (2 Chron. 24:3)

C6, D4, H3, I5
In Solomon's ______ year (ordinal number) of reign, he began to build the temple. (1 Kings 6:1)

C9, E2, F4, I8
"A man will leave his father and mother and be united to his wife, and the two will become ______ flesh." (Mark 10:7-8)

D3, E8, H9
How many daughters did Zelophehad have? (Josh. 17:3)

D6, E7, G1, H5
Ruth was the ______ woman (ordinal number) to be mentioned in the genealogy of Jesus. (Matt. 1:1-16)

8, 9, 6, 7, 2, 4, 1, 5, 3

1 = A3, D7, H1; 2 = B5, E6, I4; 3 = F2, I9; 4 = A9, E1, G7; 5 = A6, C2, F5, I1; 6 = A7, E9, H2; 7 = A1, E3, I7; 8 = C4, F7, H6;
9 = C7, D9, G6

Challenge 33

	1	2	3	4	5	6	7	8	9
A	5			6					8
B		9				3		6	7
C				9	4				
D				8	2				5
E		3							1
F		8	2						4
G	6	2							
H		5			1	4	7		
I	1			3					

A2, E4, G8
How many jars did Elijah instruct them to fill with water to pour over the burnt offering and the wood? (1 Kings 18:33)

A6, B1, I7
How many of the king's officers conspired to assassinate King Xerxes? (Esther 2:21)

A8, C6, D2
How many men from each tribe, each being the head of the house, were instructed to help with the census? (Num. 1:2-4)

B5, G3, H8
Second Corinthians is the ______ book (ordinal number) listed in the New Testament.

C3, D6, F8, I2
The ______ commandment (ordinal number) tells us that we shall not commit adultery. (Exod. 20:14)

C7, E3, I8
How many strong men did the Danites send to spy out the land? (Judges 18:1-2)

C8, F5, G9
Moses and Aaron told Pharaoh to allow the Israelites to take a ______-day journey into the wilderness to offer sacrifice to the Lord. (Exod. 5:3)

D8, F1, G6, H3
In Psalm 119, what verse asks how a young person can keep their life pure?

E6, F7, I5
How many sons did Azel have? (1 Chron. 9:44)

4, 2, 1, 8, 7, 5, 3, 9, 6

1 = B3, F4, G7; 2 = C9, E8, H4; 3 = A3, D7, H1; 4 = B7, D1, I3; 5 = B4, F6, G5; 6 = C2, D3, H9; 7 = A5, E1, G4;
8 = C1, E7, I6; 9 = A7, E5, I9

Challenge 34

	1	2	3	4	5	6	7	8	9
A	7			8				5	3
B					5				
C			1			6		2	7
D	6	2	4		1				9
E	3						8		
F						4	5		
G		6						8	
H				1			7		
I					9	2			

EASY

A2, C5, H1, I7
Into how many shares did the soldiers divide Jesus' clothes? (John 19:23)

A5, F9, G7
One handful with tranquility is better than how many handfuls with toil? (Eccles. 4:6)

B2, C7, F4, H8
The shepherd left the ninety-______ sheep to look for the missing sheep. (Matt. 18:12)

B3, F5, G6, H2
How many sons did Noah have? (Gen. 6:10)

B6, E8, I1
How many times was Peter pelted with stones? (2 Cor. 11:25)

B7, E5, I4
How many lambs was the prince instructed to sacrifice as burnt offering to the Lord? (Ezek. 46:4)

C2, F1, H5
On which day did Moses instruct Aaron and his sons to sacrifice a burnt offering to the Lord? (Lev. 9:1-2)

D8, E6, I2
How many days does the Festival of Tabernacles last? (Lev. 23:34)

E2, G3, I9
Mary was the ______ woman (ordinal number) to be named in Jesus' genealogy. (Matt. 1:1-16)

4, 2, 9, 3, 1, 6, 8, 7, 5
1 = A7, F2, G9; 2 = B1, E4, H3; 3 = C4, D7, I8; 4 = B8, E9, G4; 5 = C1, D4, H6; 6 = A3, F8, H9; 7 = B4, F3, G5; 8 = B9, D6, I3;
9 = A6, E3, G1

Challenge 35

	1	2	3	4	5	6	7	8	9
A		9		3	8				
B	2					9		4	8
C								1	
D	8								
E	7				2	5			1
F					6			5	
G	3		7				5	6	
H			9	1					4
I						6		3	

A6, F3, G4, I2
How many sins did God's people, according to Jeremiah 2:13, commit?

A7, C1, E3
The plague of boils was the ______ plague (ordinal number) God sent on Egypt. (Exod. 9:8-12)

A8, B2, D4, I9
How many years had Hebron been built before Zoan in Egypt? (Num. 13:22)

B3, C4, H1
How many smooth stones did David pick up? (1 Sam. 17:40)

B5, D3, I7
How many men escaped the battle and went to tell Abram what had happened? (Gen. 14:13)

C3, D6, F9
How many annual festivals did the Israelites have to celebrate in honor of the Lord? (Exod. 23:14)

C6, D7, F2, I1
Esau brought ______ hundred men with him to meet Jacob. (Gen. 32:6)

D5, F1, G9
Hezekiah reigned in Jerusalem for twenty-______ years. (2 Chron. 29:1)

E7, G6, H8
Multiply the number of Gospels in the Bible by 2.

2, 6, 7, 5, 1, 3, 4, 9, 8

1 = A1, F6, G2; 2 = C9, D8, H7; 3 = B7, E2, H5; 4 = A3, E4, G5; 5 = A9, D2, I5; 6 = B4, D9, H2; 7 = C5, F7, H6; 8 = C2, F4, I3;
9 = C7, E8, I4

Challenge 36

	1	2	3	4	5	6	7	8	9
A	3		7		1			6	
B									8
C			2	8		5			4
D				1	5			9	
E	9		6						
F				4					2
G		9							7
H			3			6	4		
I			1	7				8	

EASY

A4, E5, G8, I6
When Jesus died, the curtain of the temple tore into ______ pieces. (Matt. 27:51)

A6, D3, G1
According to the saying, how many months are left before the harvest? (John 4:35)

B1, E9, G4, I2
The plague that riddled the Egyptian's livestock with disease was the ______ plague (ordinal number). (Exod. 9:1-7)

B3, C5, H4
Three plus ______ is equal to the number of disciples Jesus had. (Luke 6:13)

B8, E2, H9
Sarah was ______ hundred and twenty-seven years old when she died. (Gen. 23:1)

C2, F5, G7
How many verses are there in Psalm 23?

C7, D1, F8
Balaam instructed Balak to build ______ altars. (Num. 23:1)

C8, D7, F2, G5
How many sons did Levi have? (Num. 3:17)

D6, E7, G3
In what chapter of Luke can the parable of the sower be found?

2, 4, 5, 9, 1, 6, 7, 3, 8

1 = C1, F7, G6; 2 = B7, D2, H1; 3 = B6, E4, I9; 4 = B2, E8, I5; 5 = A7, F3, H8; 6 = B4, D9, I1; 7 = B5, E6, H2; 8 = A2, F1, H5;
9 = A9, F6, I7

Challenge 37

	1	2	3	4	5	6	7	8	9
A					9				5
B	4				2	1			
C	8			7					
D	1	4	2						9
E				1				3	
F					7				
G			8		6				
H	5				3			2	6
I	9		7				5		

A1, C6, D4, G2
How many cities east of the Jordan did Moses set aside? (Deut. 4:41)

A2, E1, G8
How many years did it take to build the temple? (1 Kings 6:38)

A4, C8, D6, E7
All those who went to Egypt with Jacob, not including his sons' wives, numbered sixty-______ people. (Gen. 46:26)

A7, F9, I4
How many of Zebedee's sons became Jesus' disciples? (Mark 1:19-20)

B2, E3, F4
How many female servants did Abigail take with her when she went to David on a donkey? (1 Sam. 25:42)

B4, D5, F2, I6
In which chapter of First Samuel do the Israelites ask for a king?

C3, F6, G7
Moses told them to assign the land by lot as an inheritance because God had ordered that it be given to the ______ and a half tribes. (Num. 34:13)

C7, G9, H2
Jesus and the Father are ______. (John 10:30)

C9, F7, H3, I8
God sent swarms of flies for the ______ plague (ordinal number). (Exod. 8:20-32)

3, 7, 6, 2, 5, 8, 9, 1, 4

1 = A3, F8, I5; 2 = C2, E6, G1; 3 = B7, F3, I9; 4 = A6, E5, G4; 5 = C5, D8, G6; 6 = B3, F1, I2; 7 = B9, D7, H6; 8 = A8, E9, H7; 9 = B8, E2, H4

Challenge 38

	1	2	3	4	5	6	7	8	9
A				4	7			5	
B		8		9		5			6
C							1	2	
D	1					7			
E			8			3	6	9	
F	2								
G								4	
H	4	9					7		
I		6		3	5		2		

EASY

A1, D4, H8
According to the Sabbath laws, the Israelites were allowed to plant and harvest their crops for ______ years. (Exod. 23:10)

A3, C5, F7, G1
God turned the dust into gnats during the ______ plague (ordinal number). (Exod. 8:16-19)

A6, F9, G2, H4
For God, ______ day is the same as a thousand years. (2 Pet. 3:8)

A9, D8, G7, H5
Which chapter in Acts mentions how Saul persecuted the church?

B1, E2, G4
Even if a righteous person falls ______ times, he will rise again. (Prov. 24:16)

B5, E4, H6
How many disciples did Jesus send to find the colt? (Mark 11:1-3)

B7, D5, E9
How many beasts came up out of the sea? (Dan. 7:3)

C1, D3, G6
Issachar was the ______ son (ordinal number) of Jacob. (Gen. 29:31-30:18)

E1, F4, G9
Elizabeth remained in seclusion for ______ months. (Luke 1:24)

6, 3, 1, 8, 7, 2, 4, 9, 5

1 = B3, E5, I8; 2 = A2, D9, G3; 3 = B8, D2, H9; 4 = C3, F2, I6; 5 = C2, D7, H3; 6 = C6, F3, G5; 7 = C9, F8, I3; 8 = C4, F6, I1;
9 = A7, F5, I9

Challenge 39

	1	2	3	4	5	6	7	8	9
A	9					1			6
B	8				3		5	9	
C									
D				4			7		
E					1		8		
F	3				2				
G			6	3	4				
H		1						7	
I	2	8					4		5

A2, C5, F4, I3
Enoch was the ______ person (ordinal number) after Adam. (Jude 14)

A3, E4, F2, H5
How many husbands had the Samaritan woman at the well had in her life? (John 4:17-18)

A5, D6, H4
Add up the chapters of Philippians and Colossians. How many chapters are there altogether?

A8, C3, F9
In Daniel's vision, the goat's horn broke off and, in its place, grew ______ new horns. (Dan. 8:8)

B2, C8, E9, H6
For the ______ plague (ordinal number), God sent frogs to cover the entire country. (Exod. 8:1-15)

B4, D2, E8, I5
The Lord told the Israelites to plant and harvest their crops for ______ years. (Exod. 23:10)

C2, D9, I8
Once every ______ years, the king's fleet of ships returned carrying gold, silver and ivory, and apes and baboons. (1 Kings 10:22)

C7, D1, G9
How many bags of coins did the servant who buried his master's money receive? (Matt. 25:18)

E3, F7, G2, H9
In what verse in First Chronicles chapter 3 is David's daughter, Tamar, first mentioned?

9 = C4, D5, I6

1 = B3, F8, I4; 2 = A4, D3, G7; 3 = A7, E6, H3; 4 = B6, E2, H1; 5 = C6, D8, G1; 6 = C1, F6, H7; 7 = B9, E1, G6; 8 = C9, F3, G8;

7, 5, 8, 4, 2, 6, 3, 1, 9

Challenge 40

EASY

	1	2	3	4	5	6	7	8	9
A			7	8		6		4	
B					4	3			
C			5					8	6
D						7			
E	5						7		4
F	2						1		
G		1			6		5		3
H			9	2		8			
I		3						9	

A1, B4, D5, E2
Take Enosh's age when he fathered Kenan and divide it by 10. (Gen. 5:9)

A2, B7, E5, I3
How many messengers did John the Baptist send to Jesus? (Luke 7:18-19)

A5, D8, H2
How many basins for washing was placed on the south side? (2 Chron. 4:6)

A9, C4, D3, I5
God turned the water of the Nile River into blood for the ______ plague (ordinal number). (Exod. 7:14)

B8, H9, I1
How many years of famine did Joseph warn would come upon Egypt? (Gen. 41:30)

C1, E8, F3
How many years did the peace between Syria (or Aram) and Israel last? (1 Kings 22:1)

D2, E4, I7
How many sheep were prepared for Nehemiah every day? (Neh. 5:18)

D7, F5, G1
Ishmael and ______ of his men escaped from Johanan. (Jer. 41:15)

F6, H7, I4
The horns that replaced the one that had broken off represent ______ kingdoms. (Dan. 8:22)

9, 2, 5, 1, 7, 3, 6, 8, 4

1 = B1, E6, H8; 2 = C6, D9, G8; 3 = A7, D4, H5; 4 = C2, D1, G3; 5 = B9, F4, I6; 6 = B3, F8, H1; 7 = C5, F2, G4; 8 = B2, E3, I9;
9 = C7, F9, G6

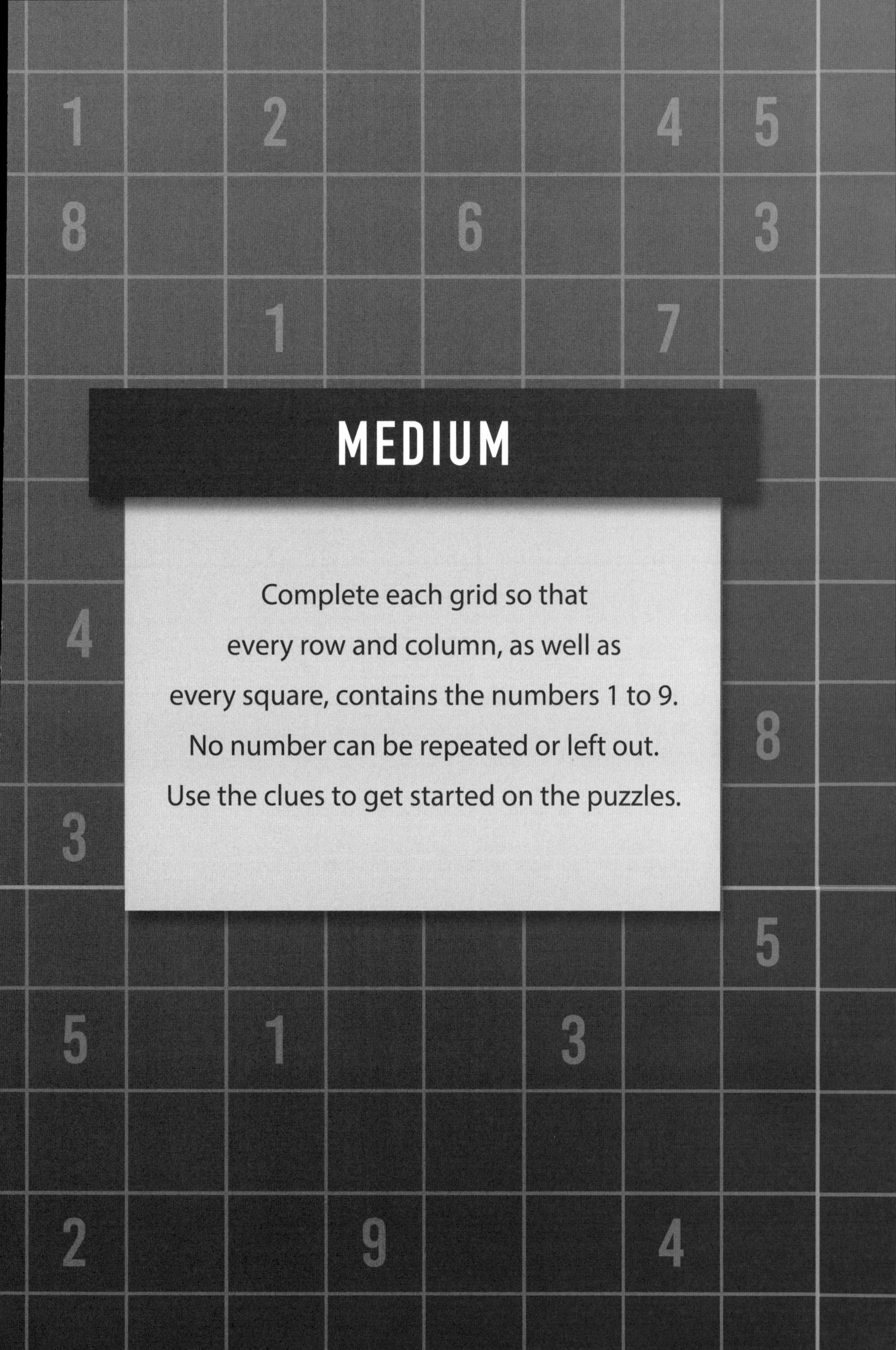

MEDIUM

Complete each grid so that every row and column, as well as every square, contains the numbers 1 to 9. No number can be repeated or left out. Use the clues to get started on the puzzles.

Challenge 41

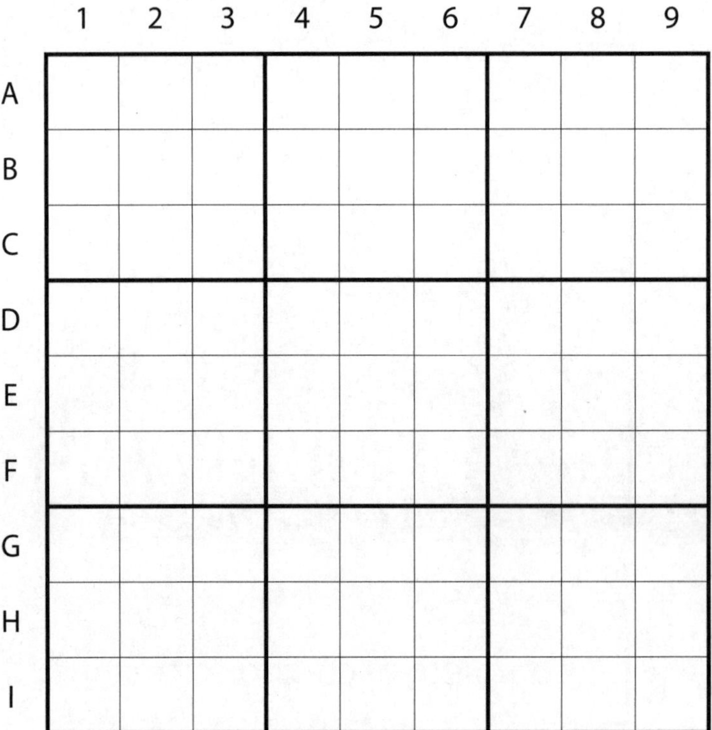

A3, D8, G5
How many days did the Israelites travel through the desert without finding water? (Exod. 15:22-23)

A5, D4, H1
How many coins did the woman in Luke 15:8-10 lose?

A6, E5, F1, I3
Galatians is the ______ book (ordinal number) listed in the New Testament.

A7, D3, F6, G4
How many men did King Nebuchadnezzar see walking around unharmed in the fiery oven? (Dan. 3:25)

A9, E8, I6
How many wings did each of the living creatures in John's vision have? (Rev. 4:8)

B3, C7, G2, I9
How many of Samson's braids did Delilah shave off? (Judges 16:19)

B4, F5, H6
How many Amorite kings joined forces to attack Gibeon? (Josh. 10:5)

B9, D6, F3, I4
How many letters did Paul write to the Thessalonians?

C1, E4, G9
How many years were the Israelites forced to serve Cushan-Rishathaim, king of Mesopotamia? (Judges 3:8)

3, 1, 9, 4, 6, 7, 5, 2, 8

1 = B8, C3, E2, F9, G6, I7; 2 = A1, C5, E7, G8, H2; 3 = B7, C6, E1, F4, H9, I2; 4 = B5, C2, E9, H8, I1; 5 = A2, C9, D7, E3, G1, I8; 6 = B1, C4, D5, F2, G3, H7; 7 = A4, D1, E6, F8, H5; 8 = A8, B6, D2, F7, H3, I5; 9 = B2, C8, D9, G7, H4

Challenge 42

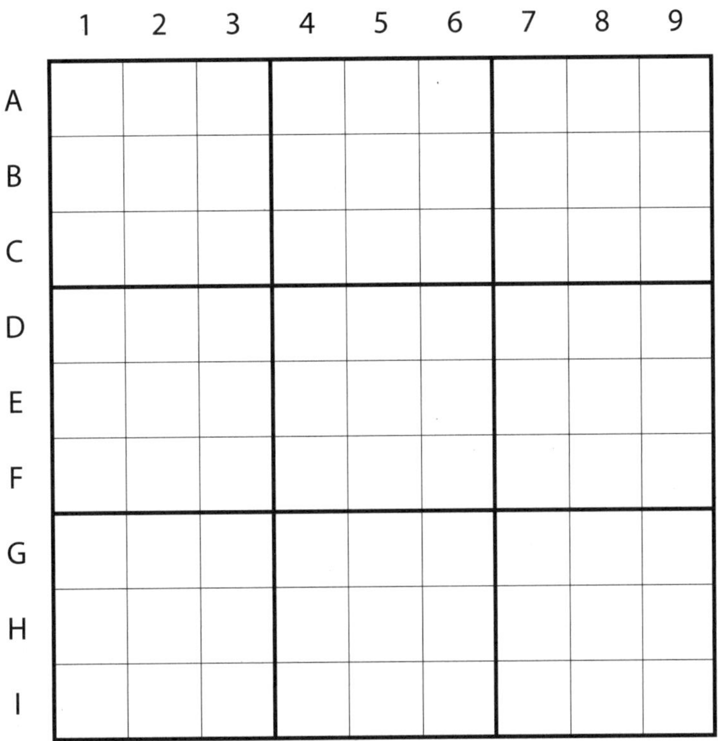

MEDIUM

A1, D4, H3, I6
In the Beatitudes how many blessings are listed? (Matt. 5:3-11)

A4, C9, E5, F8, G2
The Israelites were allowed to work ______ days per week. (Exod. 20:9)

A5, C2, E1, F4, H8
How many sons did Hannah, Samuel's mother, have according to First Samuel 2:18-21?

A7, D5, G9, H2
The plague of hail was the ______ plague (ordinal number). (Exod. 9:13-35)

A9, B1, F5, G3
How many chapters are in the Old Testament book Joel?

B2, D6, H7, I1
How many sons did Abigail have according to First Chronicles 2:17?

B4, D9, F3, I5
How many loaves of bread did Jesus use to feed the 5,000 people? (Matt. 14:17)

B8, D3, G5, I2
How many oxen did Moses give to the Merarites for their work? (Num. 7:8)

D8, E2, G1, I9
Jesus told Peter, "Before the rooster crows ______, you will deny Me." (Mark 14:72)

6 = B3, D1, H6, I7; 7 = B6, C3, E8, F1, I4; 8 = A6, C1, E4, F7, H9; 9 = B5, C7, E9, F2, G8

1 = A8, C5, E3, F9, G4; 2 = A3, B7, C4, F6, H5; 3 = C6, D2, E7, H4, I8; 4 = B9, D7, G6, I3; 5 = A2, C8, E6, G7, H1;

9, 6, 4, 7, 3, 1, 5, 8, 2

Challenge 43

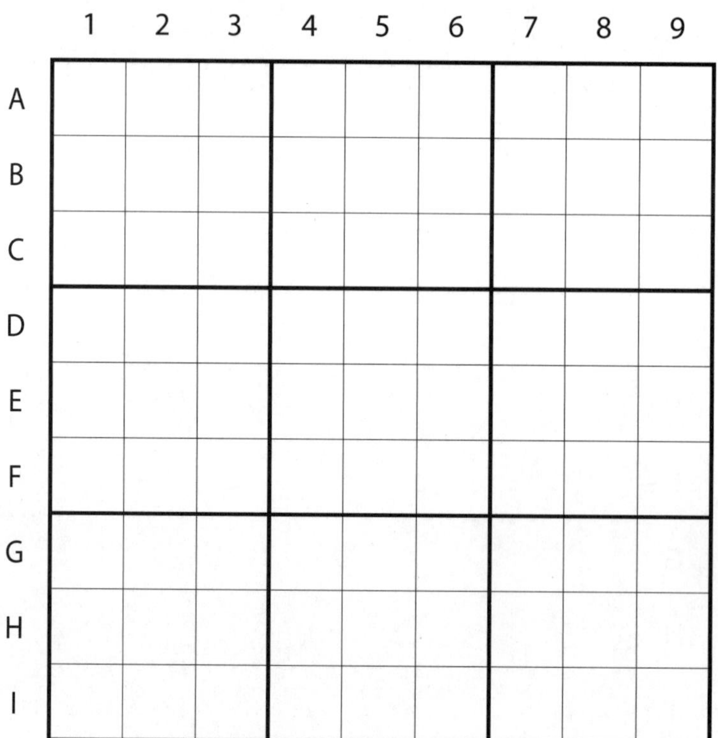

A4, F5, G6, I9
How many people lived in the Garden of Eden? (Gen. 2)

A9, D8, E4, F1, I5
In how many divine Persons does God exist? (1 John 5:7-8)

B1, C7, E9, H3
How many daughters did Leah have? (Gen. 34:1)

B5, E6, G2, H8
How many kingdoms are represented by the new horns? (Dan. 8:22)

B7, F6, G8, I2
On what day were the Israelites supposed to gather and prepare twice as much bread, called manna? (Exod. 16:5)

B8, D2, E5, H9
How much bigger was Benjamin's portion than his brothers? (Gen. 43:34)

C1, D3, G7, I6
On what day did Abidan bring his offering? (Num. 7:60)

C4, E7, F3, H5, I1
How many chapters are there altogether in First and Second Peter?

D5, E3, F8, H6
How many pairs of clean animals were Noah instructed to take onto the ark? (Gen. 7:2)

6 = A3, C5, D9, E1, H4; 7 = A2, B4, C9, G1, I7; 8 = A8, B2, D6, G9; 9 = A5, B9, E8, F4, H2

1 = A6, D4, F2, G5, I8; 2 = B3, C8, D7, E2, H1; 3 = B6, C2, G3, H7; 4 = A7, C3, D1, F9, I4; 5 = A1, C6, F7, G4, I3;

2, 3, 1, 4, 6, 5, 9, 8, 7

Challenge 44

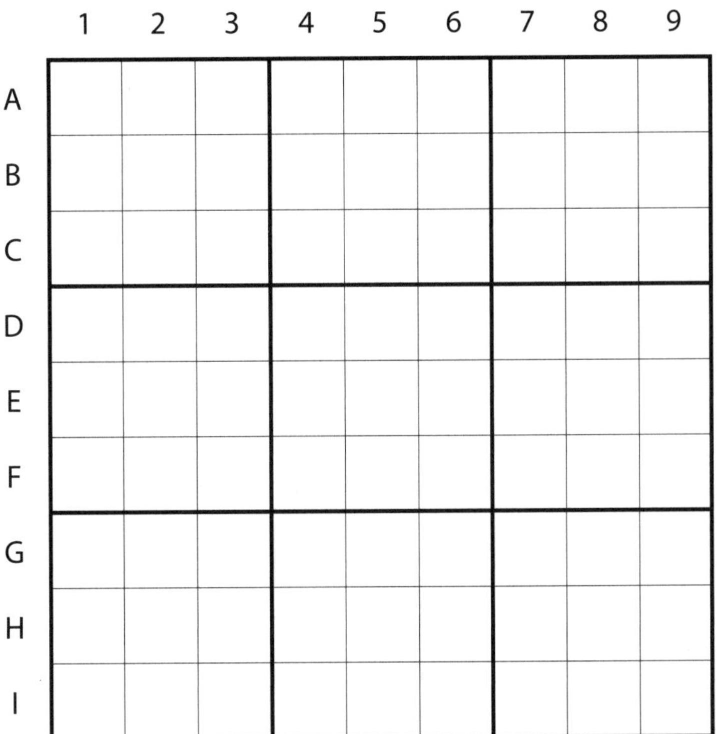

MEDIUM

A5, G3, I8
How many chapters are in the Old Testament book Micah?

A8, B1, D9, G5, I7
How many years were the Israelites allowed to sow their fields and harvest their crops? (Exod. 23:10)

B3, C6, G7, I2
Ruth is the ______ woman (ordinal number) to be listed in the genealogy of Jesus. (Matt. 1:1-16)

B4, C8, F2, G9
How many verses does Psalm 130 have?

B6, D2, G8, H3
Enosh was ______ multiplied by 10 years old when he fathered Kenan. (Gen. 5:9)

B9, F8, H7
How many things did Jacob ask Laban to do for him as payment for tending his flocks? (Gen. 30:31)

C3, E9, I6
How many years after Solomon became king of Israel did they start building the temple? (1 Kings 6:1)

C7, F3, H9, I1
How many of the king's officers conspired to assassinate King Xerxes? (Esther 2:21)

D3, E5, F7, H4
How many brothers did the rich man in the parable have? (Luke 16:28)

7, 6, 3, 8, 9, 1, 4, 2, 5

1 = A2, C5, D6, E1, G4, I3; 2 = A4, B2, D5, E8, G6; 3 = A9, D8, E4, F1, H5; 4 = A7, B5, D1, F4, G2, H8; 5 = A6, B8, C2, G1, I9;
6 = C4, E3, F6, H2; 7 = B7, C1, D4, E2, F9, H6; 8 = A3, D7, E6, H1, I5; 9 = A1, C9, E7, F5, I4

Challenge 45

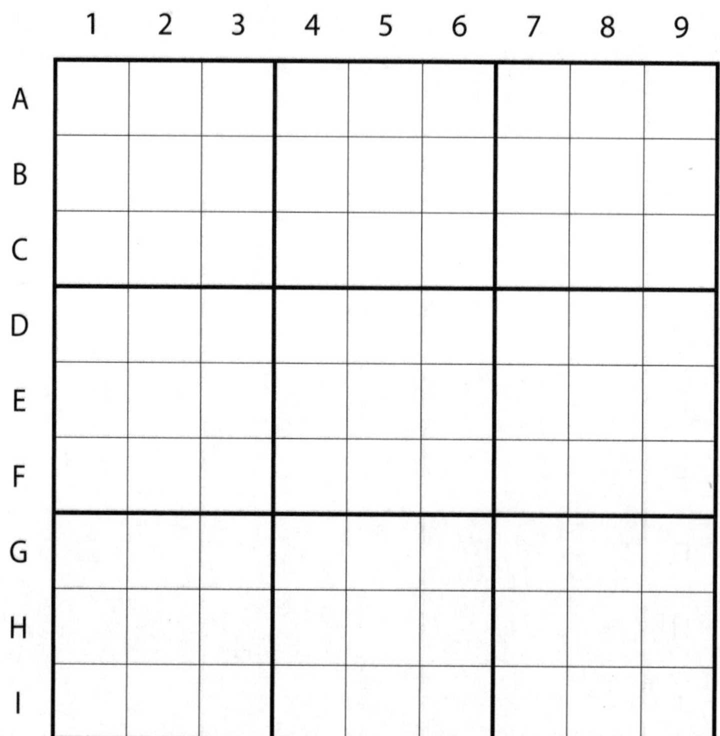

A1, E4, F2, G6
How many people were on the ark? (Gen. 7:13)

A2, C4, D5, F8, G3
How many baskets did the chief baker have on his head in his dream? (Gen. 40:16)

A5, E6, F3
Rahab was the ______ woman listed in Jesus' genealogy? (Matt. 1:1-16)

A7, F1, G4, H9
How many talents did the third servant in the parable receive? (Matt. 25:14-15)

A9, D4, H8, I1
How many plagues did the angels bring? (Rev. 15:1)

B6, E2, I4
How many loaves of bread were to be placed in each row on the golden table of the tabernacle? (Lev. 24:5-6)

C1, F9, I6
In what verse in First Chronicles chapter 3 is David's daughter, Tamar, first mentioned?

C3, E9, F4, I2
How many cities in Egypt would speak the language of Canaan and swear allegiance to the Lord Almighty? (Isa. 19:18)

C8, D2, I5
The concubine left him and went to her father's house in Bethlehem where she stayed for ______ months. (Judges 19:1-2)

8, 3, 2, 1, 7, 6, 9, 5, 4

1 = B5, C2, D6, E8, I3; 2 = B1, C7, D9, G2, H4, I8; 3 = B9, E1, H6, I7; 4 = A4, B3, E7, F6, G9, H1; 5 = A6, B7, D1, G8, H5; 6 = A3, C9, D8, F5, G1, H7; 7 = B2, C6, E3, F7, G5; 8 = B8, C5, D7, H3, I9; 9 = A8, B4, D3, E5, G7, H2

Challenge 46

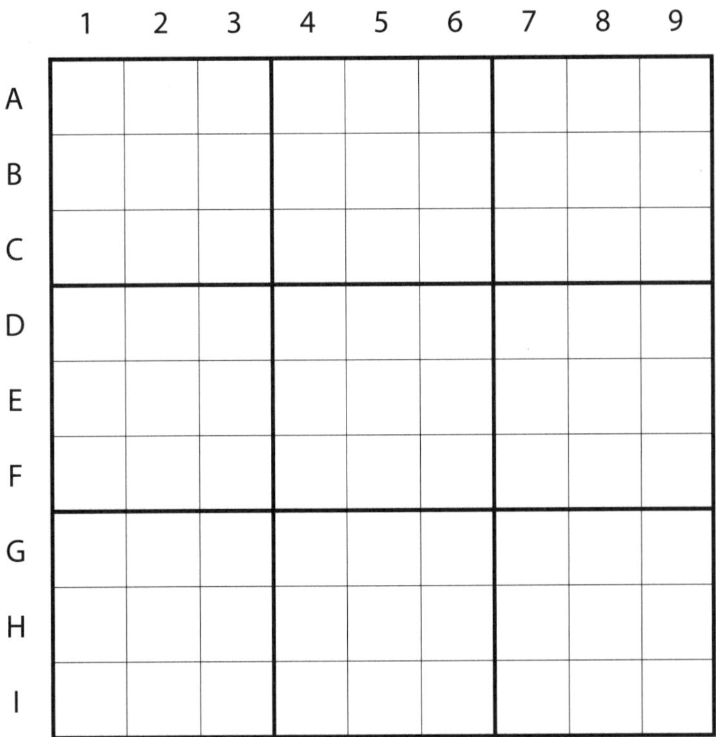

MEDIUM

A1, B7, E2, H8
How many days after Jacob had fled was Laban told? (Gen. 31:22)

A4, C2, E5, F1, G6
How many months were the locusts allowed to torment the people without the seal of God on their forehead? (Rev. 9:1-5)

A7, E9, F5, G2
How many times did Joseph and Mary have to flee with baby Jesus? (Matt. 2:14-21)

A8, F7, I2
All those who went to Egypt with Jacob, not including his sons' wives, numbered sixty-______ people. (Gen. 46:26)

A9, H1
Issachar was the ______ son (ordinal number) of Jacob. (Gen. 29:31-30:18)

B2, E8, G7, I5
The ______ commandment (ordinal number) tells us to keep the Sabbath day holy. (Exod. 20:8-11)

B3, D2, E7, G1, H9
Enoch was the ______ person (ordinal number) after Adam. (Jude 14)

B6, D4, H2, I9
One handful with tranquility is better than how many handfuls with toil? (Eccles. 4:6)

C5, G8, H6
How many days, divided by 5, was Jesus tempted by the devil? (Matt. 4:1-2)

3, 5, 1, 6, 9, 4, 7, 2, 8

1 = B1, C6, D3, H4, I8; 2 = A3, C7, E1, F8, G5; 3 = C4, D5, F9, G3, I6; 4 = A6, C9, D1, F4, H3; 5 = B8, D9, H7, I3;
6 = B4, C1, D6, E3, G9, H5; 7 = A5, C8, F6, I4; 8 = A2, B9, D7, E4, F3, I1; 9 = B5, C3, D8, E6, F2, G4, I7

Challenge 47

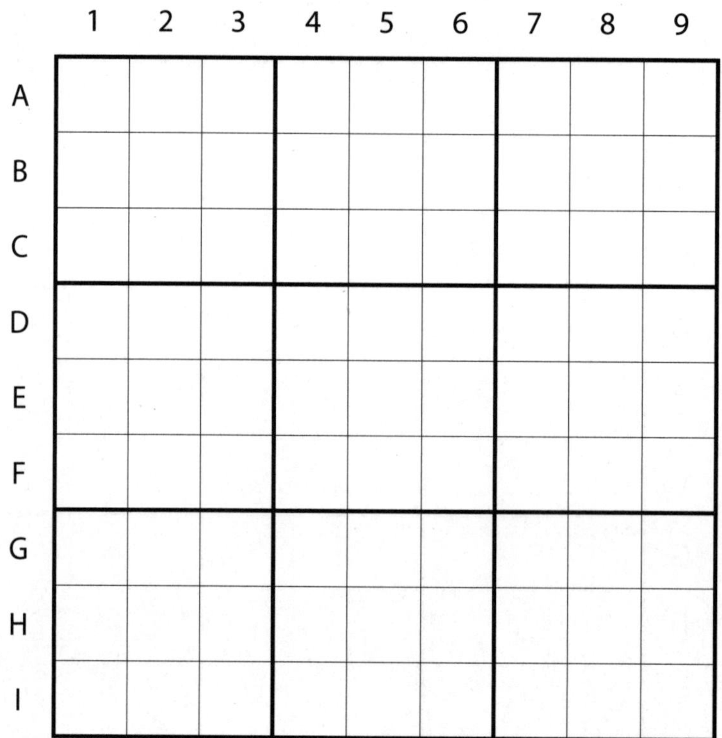

A1, F5, H2, I4
Take the number of days Jonah spent in the belly of the fish and multiply it by 3. (Matt. 12:40)

A3, D5, G8, H6
How many verses are there in Psalm 23?

A4, F8, G6, I3
How many chapters are in the New Testament book James?

A7, G5, I8
How many soldiers pierced Jesus' side with a spear? (John 19:34)

B3, E1, I2
The Lord instructed Moses to take ______ onyx stones and engrave the names of the sons of Israel on them. (Exod. 28:9)

B7, C5, D8, G3
How many groups did Abimelech divide his soldiers in to ambush Shechem? (Judges 9:34)

C3, D4, E8, H7
How many decks were there in Noah's ark? (Gen. 6:16)

D6, E9
How many days did Paul and the others stay with the disciples in Tyre? (Acts 21:3-4)

E3, F4, I6
Adam lived another ______ hundred years after Seth was born. (Gen. 5:4)

9, 6, 5, 1, 2, 4, 3, 7, 8

1 = B1, C6, D2, E4, F9, H3; 2 = A8, C4, D9, F6, G7, H5; 3 = A6, B9, F2, G1, I5; 4 = A2, E6, F1, H4, I9; 5 = B2, C7, D1, E5, H9;
6 = B4, C9, E2, F7, I1; 7 = A5, B8, C2, F3, G4, H1, I7; 8 = A9, B5, C1, D7, G2, H8; 9 = B6, C8, D3, E7, G9

Challenge 48

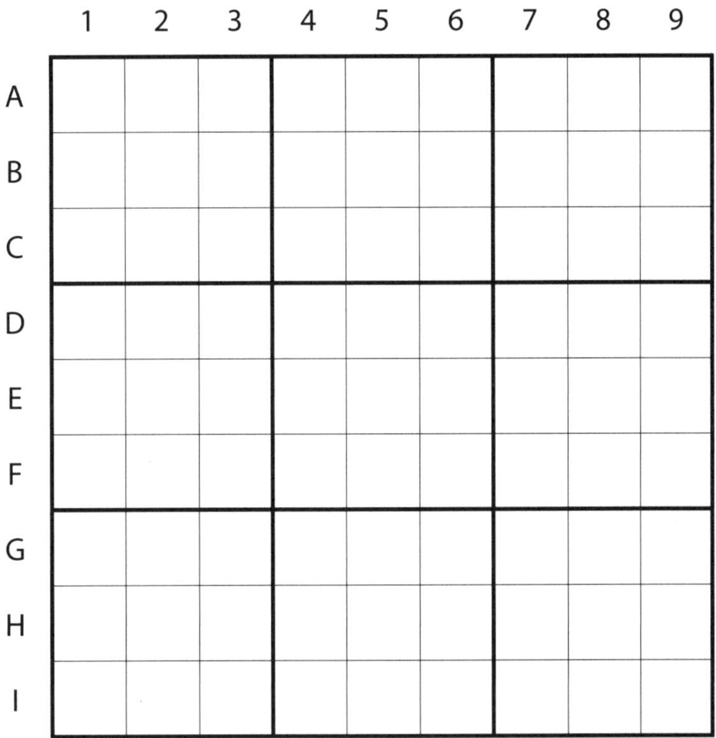

A4, E3, I8
The plague of boils was the ______ plague (ordinal number) God sent on Egypt. (Exod. 9:8-12)

A6, F1, H3
In what month of the second year of Darius, did the word of the Lord come to the prophet Zechariah? (Zech. 1:1)

A7, E9, F5, G1
How many times did Paul beg the Lord to remove the thorn from his side? (2 Cor. 12:8)

B2, C6, E5, I7
How many chapters are in the Old Testament book Obadiah?

B7, F4, G3
How many stronger nations were there that God promised to help the Israelites drive out of the land? (Deut. 7:1-2)

B8, C4, D7, I2
How many young women did not have enough oil in their lamps? (Matt. 25:1-13)

C1, E8, G2, H7, I6
How many sins did God's people, according to Jeremiah 2:13, commit? (Jer. 2:13)

D1, E4, F8
Three plus ______ is equal to the number of disciples Jesus had. (Luke 6:13)

F2, G7, H4
How many tassels were to be sewn onto the garment? (Deut. 22:12)

6, 8, 3, 1, 7, 5, 2, 9, 4

1 = A8, D3, F9, G4, H1; 2 = A9, B4, D5, F3; 3 = B6, C3, D2, H8, I4; 4 = A5, B3, C8, D9, E6, I1; 5 = A3, E1, F6, G9, H5;
6 = B1, C9, D6, F7, G5, H2; 7 = A1, C5, D8, E2, H6, I9; 8 = B9, C2, D4, E7, G8, I5; 9 = A2, B5, C7, G6, H9, I3

MEDIUM

Challenge 49

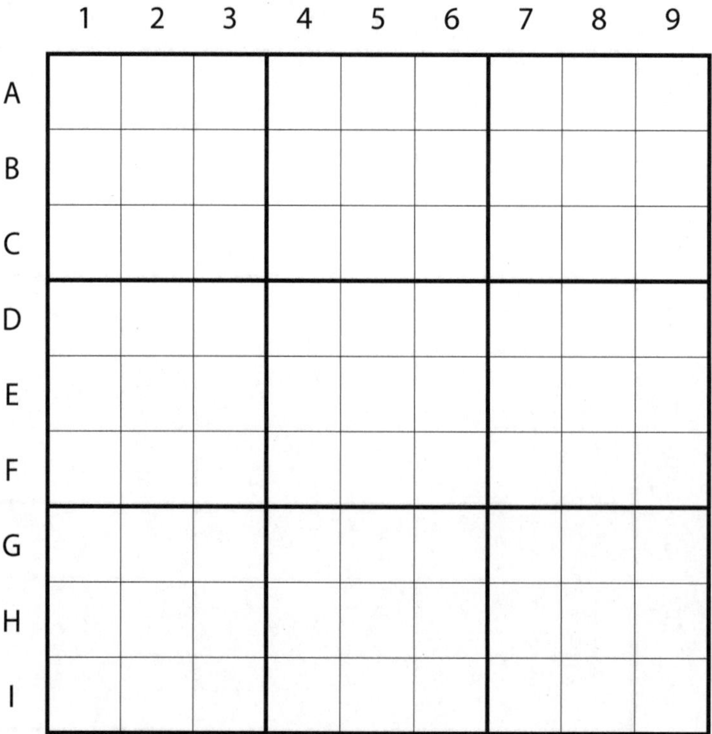

A1, D4, E2, I3
How many of his brothers did Joseph introduce to Pharaoh? (Gen. 47:2)

A4, D5, H2, I6
How many younger brothers did Joseph have? (Gen. 35:16-20)

A5, E6, F1, I8
How many verses are in Psalm 101?

A8, C4, G2, H9
Hezekiah reigned in Jerusalem for twenty-______ years. (2 Chron. 29:1)

A9, B1, G3
How many brothers did David have? (1 Sam. 16:10-12)

B7, E5, F3
How many times did Jesus leave His sleeping disciples to pray in the Garden of Gethsemane? (Matt. 26:39-44)

B9, D7, E3, G8
If you added up the chapters in Obadiah and Jude, how many chapters would you have altogether?

C2, E8, G1, H4
How many lambs was the prince instructed to sacrifice as burnt offering to the Lord? (Ezek. 46:4)

C8, G5, I1
Peter was put in prison and guarded by ______ squads of soldiers. (Acts 12:4-5)

5, 1, 8, 9, 7, 3, 2, 6, 4

1 = B8, C3, E1, F9, G7; 2 = A6, C1, F4, H5, I2; 3 = A2, C6, D8, G9, H1, I4; 4 = A3, B4, D6, E9, F2, H7; 5 = B5, C9, F7, G6, H8; 6 = A7, B6, D3, F5, I9; 7 = C5, D2, E4, F8, H6, I7; 8 = B2, C7, D9, G4, H3; 9 = B3, D1, E7, F6, I5

Challenge 50

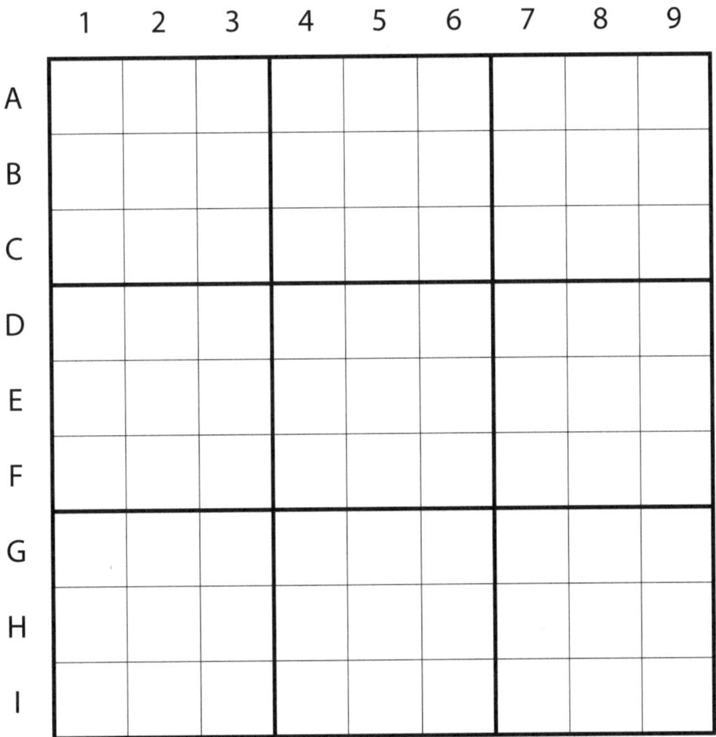

MEDIUM

A1, D7, E2, G9
When Jesus died, the curtain of the temple tore into ______ pieces. (Matt. 27:51)

A5, B2, F3, H7
How many sons did Azel have? (1 Chron. 9:44)

A7, B4, D6, H1
The shepherd left the ninety-______ sheep to look for the missing sheep. (Matt. 18:12)

A8, D9, H4
How many times will the person who kills Cain be punished? (Gen. 4:15)

B7, D4, E3, F8
How many chapters are in the Old Testament book Ruth?

B9, F4, G8
Which of the ten commandments says you shall not steal? (Exod. 20:1-17)

C1, F5, H6, I2
How many ribs did God take from Adam to make Eve? (Gen. 2:21)

C4, E5, H8
How many Amorite kings joined forces to attack Gibeon? (Josh. 10:5)

C7, G4, I8
After ______ years, Paul went up to Jerusalem to see Peter. (Gal. 1:18)

2, 6, 9, 7, 4, 8, 1, 5, 3
1 = A4, B8, D3, E9, G7; 2 = B5, C8, F6, H3, I4; 3 = A3, B6, D5, E1, F9, H2; 4 = A6, C2, G1, H9, I5; 5 = A9, B1, D2, F7, G3, I6;
6 = C9, D8, E4, G6, I1; 7 = B3, C5, E6, F1, G2, I7; 8 = A2, C6, D1, E7, H5, I3; 9 = C3, E8, F2, G5, I9

Challenge 51

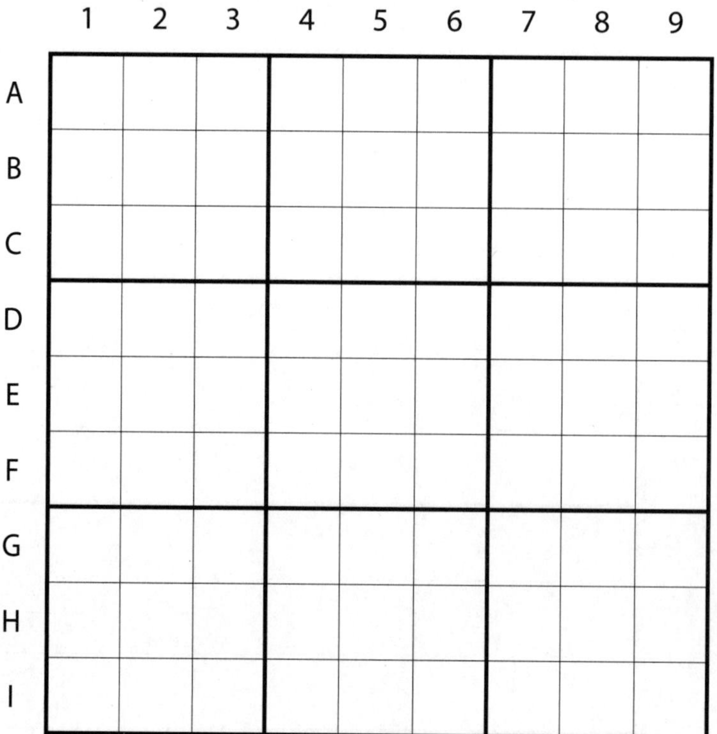

A1, B7, G9, H4
Every how many years is considered a Sabbath rest? (Lev. 25:4)

A2, C4, G7, I5
Joseph interpreted the dreams of two men while in prison. Of those men, how many were set free? (Gen. 40:1-23)

A4, E2, G5, I9
In Psalm 119, what verse asks how a young person can keep their life pure?

A5, D9, E6, F3
How many women appear in the book of the genealogy of Jesus Christ? (Matt. 1:1-16)

A9, B6, F5
How many rooms did the tabernacle have? (Heb. 9:2-3)

B2, C5, F9, H6, I1
How many Christian virtues are named in 1 Corinthians 13:13?

B4, D5, F8, H2
How many groups were Ithamar's descendants divided into? (1 Chron. 24:4)

C1, E3, I8
The ______ commandment (ordinal number) tells us that we shall not murder. (Exod. 20:13)

F4, G1, H9
How many rows of precious stones were to be set in the breastplate? (Exod. 28:15-17)

7, 1, 9, 5, 2, 3, 8, 6, 4

1 = B8, D6, E9, F1, H3; 2 = C2, D1, E8, G3, H7, I4; 3 = A7, D3, E4, G8; 4 = A8, B5, C3, D2, E7, I6; 5 = B1, C7, G4, H8, I2;
6 = A6, B9, D4, F7, G2, H5; 7 = C6, D8, E5, F2, I3; 8 = A3, C9, E1, G6, I7; 9 = B3, C8, D7, F6, H1

Challenge 52

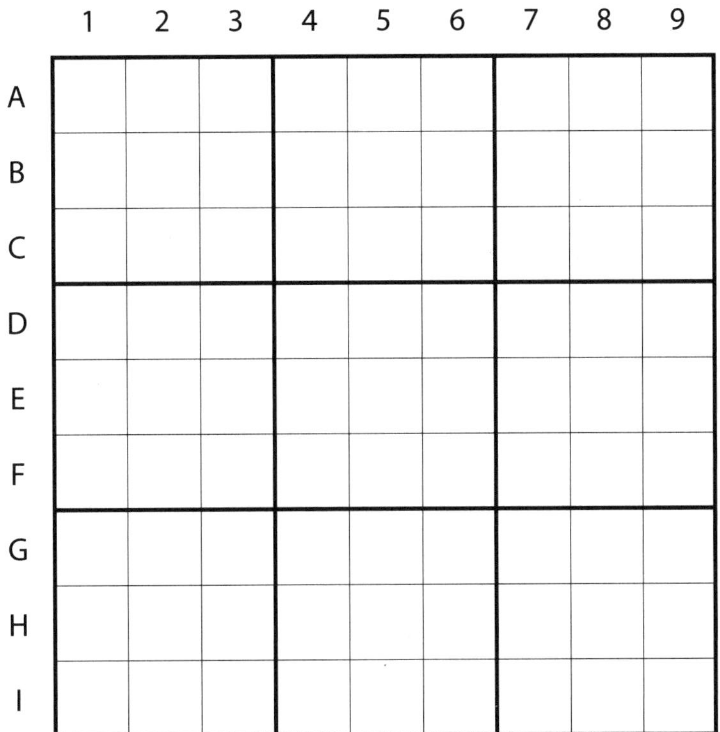

MEDIUM

A3, F9, H5
How many small copper coins did the poor widow give as an offering? (Mark 12:41-44)

A4, B9, E8, G3
How many sons did Abraham's brother Nahor and his wife, Milcah, have? (Gen. 22:20-23)

A8, C6, H9, I4
How many daughters did David have? (1 Chron. 3:9)

B1, D3, G8, H2
How many months did Moses' mother hide him? (Heb. 11:23)

B4, C8, F3
What chapter in Luke talks about Jesus' transfiguration?

C3, D1, F8
How many descendants did Shekaniah have? (1 Chron. 3:22)

C5, E2, F4
How old was Joash when he became king? (2 Kings 11:21)

D9, E4, G7
How many anchors did the sailors drop because they were afraid that the ship might hit some rocks? (Acts 27:29)

F6, H8, I3
How many kings are listed in Genesis 14:2?

2, 8, 1, 3, 9, 6, 7, 4, 5

1 = B2, D7, E3, F5, G1; 2 = B6, C7, D4, E1, G2, I8; 3 = A9, C4, E6, F7, I5; 4 = A5, B8, C1, F2, H3, I6; 5 = A1, B5, C9, D2, E7, G4; 6 = A6, B7, E5, G9, H4, I2; 7 = A7, B3, D8, G6, H1, I9; 8 = C2, D5, F1, H6, I7; 9 = A2, D6, E9, G5, H7, I1

Challenge 53

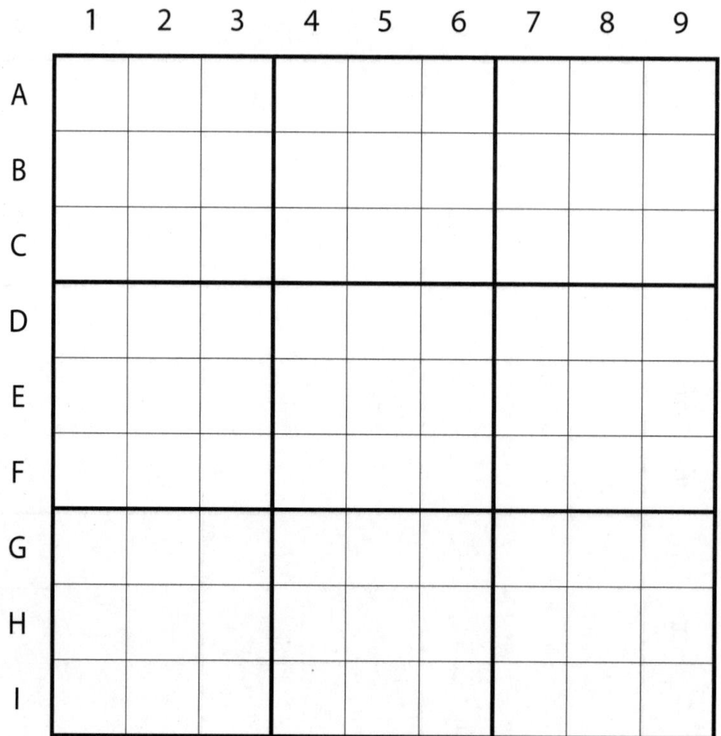

A1, B5, F8, G9
In what chapter of Acts do Ananias and Sapphira pay the price for lying to the Holy Spirit?

A2, B9, D5, E8, F1
How many of Zebedee's sons became Jesus' disciples? (Mark 1:19)

A7, C5, H3
First Samuel is the ______ book (ordinal number) listed in the Old Testament.

A9, B3, E7, F6
When the Assyrians invade the Israelites' land, how many commanders or princes will rise up against them? (Mic. 5:5)

B2, D9, G5
How many angels did John notice in Revelation 8:2?

B6, E3, I4
How many winds of heaven were stirring up the sea in Daniel's vision? (Dan. 7:2)

B7, C1, G3, H5
How many years did Jephthah serve as judge? (Judges 12:7)

E5, G8, I1
How many sons did Noah have? (Gen. 6:10)

G6, H7, I2
How many chapters are in the New Testament book Second John?

5, 2, 9, 8, 7, 4, 6, 3, 1

1 = A5, B8, C3, D4, E1, F9; 2 = C6, G7, H4, I3; 3 = A3, B4, C9, D2, F7, H6; 4 = A8, C2, D7, F5, G1, H9; 5 = C7, D3, E4, H2, I6; 6 = A6, D8, E2, F4, I9; 7 = A4, C8, E6, F3, H1, I7; 8 = C4, D1, G2, H8, I5; 9 = B1, D6, E9, F2, G4, I8

Challenge 54

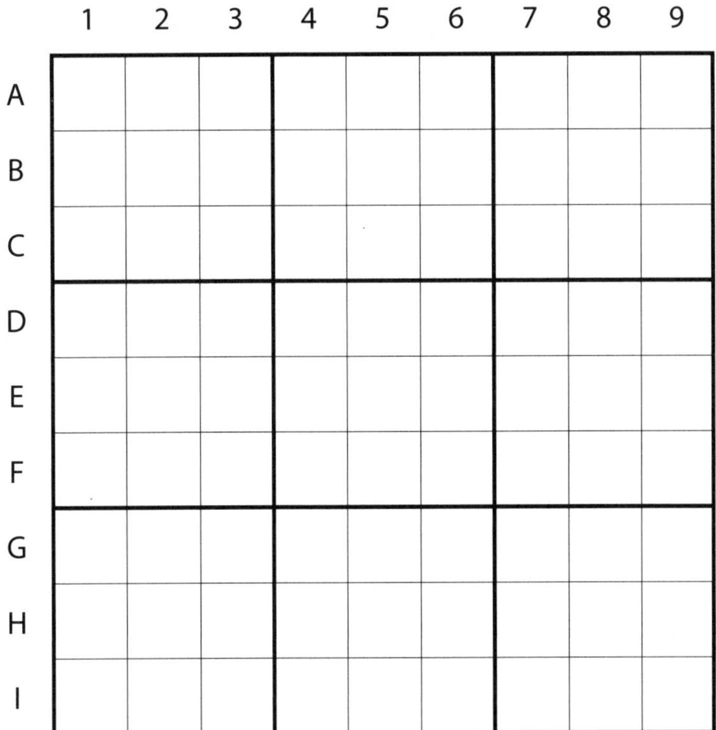

MEDIUM

A1, E8, G2, H9
How many gates were on each side of the wall? (Rev. 21:13)

A4, C3, E5, F7
Moses was instructed to select ______ towns to be the Israelites' cities of refuge, to which a person who had accidentally killed someone could flee. (Num. 35:9-13)

A7, B4, H3, I6
How many bulls were to be sacrificed on the fifth day? (Num. 29:25-27)

B1, D8, H7
How many women did Lamech marry? (Gen. 4:19)

B3, D4, G7
What verse in Psalm 23 starts with the words "The Lord is my Shepherd"?

B6, C8, H4, I1
How many gold rings were cast and placed on the ark? (Exod. 37:3)

B7, D3, G1, I8
How many years was Abdon the leader of Israel? (Judges 12:13-14)

D1, E6, H5
How old was Mephibosheth when he learned that his father, Jonathan, was dead? (2 Sam. 4:4)

E3, G4, H8
How many female lambs did Abraham give to Abimelech to prove that he had dug the well called Beersheba? (Gen. 21:28-31)

3, 6, 9, 2, 1, 4, 8, 5, 7

1 = A8, C6, E9, F1, H2, I5; 2 = A6, C9, E2, F4, G5, I3; 3 = B5, C7, D6, F3, I4; 4 = A3, D5, E7, F2, G9; 5 = A9, B2, C4, F8, G3, I7;
6 = B8, D2, G6, H1, I9; 7 = A5, B9, C1, D7, F6, I2; 8 = A2, C5, E4, F9, H6; 9 = C2, D9, E1, F5, G8

Challenge 55

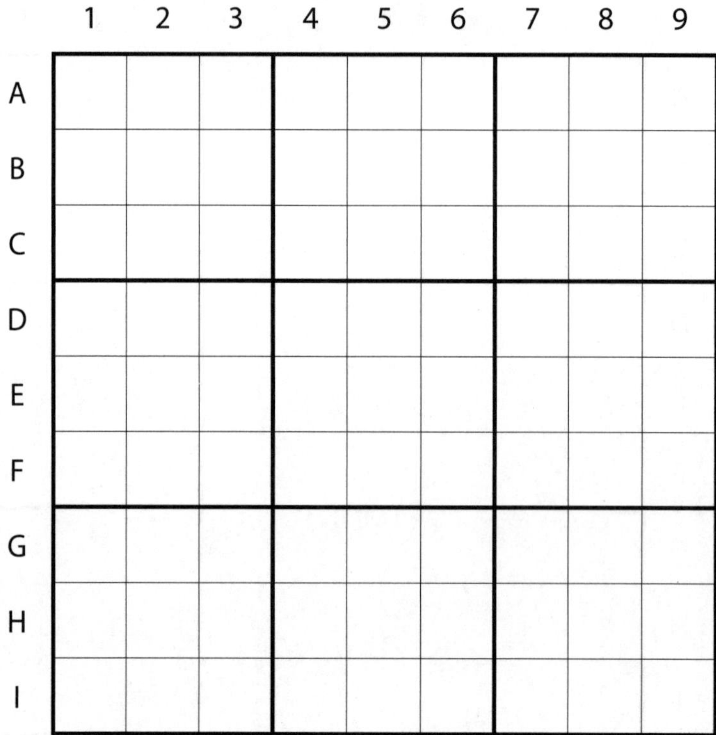

A4, C3, F7, I1
How many branches were to extend from the sides of the lampstand? (Exod. 25:32)

A6, B9, D2, H4
Into how many riverheads did the main river which flowed out of Eden separate? (Gen. 2:10)

A8, C6, F1
How many books of the law are there in the Bible?

B1, E5, I9
Seth was ______ hundred and twelve years old when he died. (Gen. 5:8)

C2, D7, H8
In what chapter of Revelation are the seven trumpets first mentioned?

C7, G4, I8
How many disciples did Jesus send to find the colt? (Mark 11:1-3)

C8, D4, G3, I6
How many woes are listed in Matthew 23:13-26?

C9, D3, E8, F6
How many things does David ask of God in Psalm 27:4?

D1, E6, H9
How many disciples did Jesus take with Him to the mountain where He was transfigured? (Matt. 17:1-2)

6 = B8, D5, E2, G9, H6; 7 = A2, B5, E1, F9, H7; 8 = A9, B6, E3, F4, G1, I5; 9 = A7, C4, D8, F3, G6, H2

1 = A1, B4, G7, H5, I2; 2 = A5, B3, D6, E9, F2, H1; 3 = A3, B7, C5, F8, G2, I4; 4 = C1, E7, F5, G8, I3; 5 = B2, D9, E4, G5, H3, I7;

6, 4, 5, 9, 8, 2, 7, 1, 3

Challenge 56

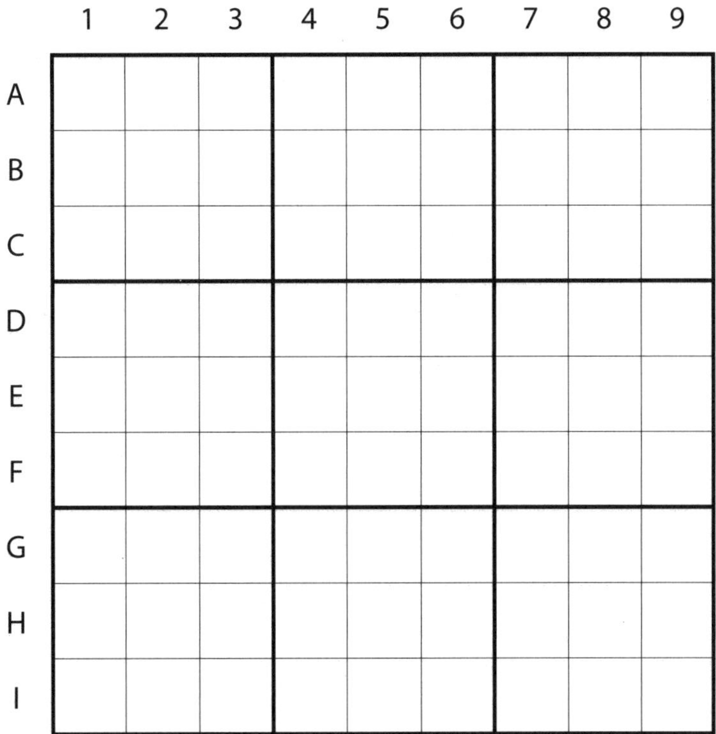

A2, H7, I1
How many boats were left by the water's edge? (Luke 5:2)

A3, D7, F4, G2
How many tables were there in the room used to prepare animal sacrifices? (Ezek. 40:41)

A4, B9, C2, E6
The Lord instructed Moses to take two onyx stones and engrave the names of the sons of Israel on them. ______ names on one stone and the remaining ______ on the other. (Exod. 28:9-10)

A5, B3, F9, I8
How many members of Saul's family were still alive when David asked after them? (2 Sam. 9:1-3)

A6, C1, F8, G4
How many years did it take Solomon to build the temple? (1 Kings 6:38)

A8, F1, H5
How many times did Peter betray Jesus? (Mark 14:66-72)

B1, F2, G8, I4
How many chapters are in the Old Testament book Jonah?

B2, E8, F6, H9
On what day did God create the fish and birds? (Gen. 1:20-23)

B8, C5, E4
How many sons did David have who were not born in Hebron or Jerusalem? (1 Chron. 3:1-9)

2, 8, 6, 1, 7, 3, 4, 5, 9

1 = C7, D6, E2, G1, H4; 2 = B4, C8, D9, E3, F5, G6; 3 = B6, C3, D4, E9, G7, I2; 4 = A9, C6, D5, E7, H3; 5 = A7, C4, D1, G3, I5; 6 = D8, F3, G5, H1, I7; 7 = B7, D3, E5, H2, I9; 8 = B5, C9, E1, H8, I6; 9 = A1, D2, F7, G9, H6, I3

MEDIUM

Challenge 57

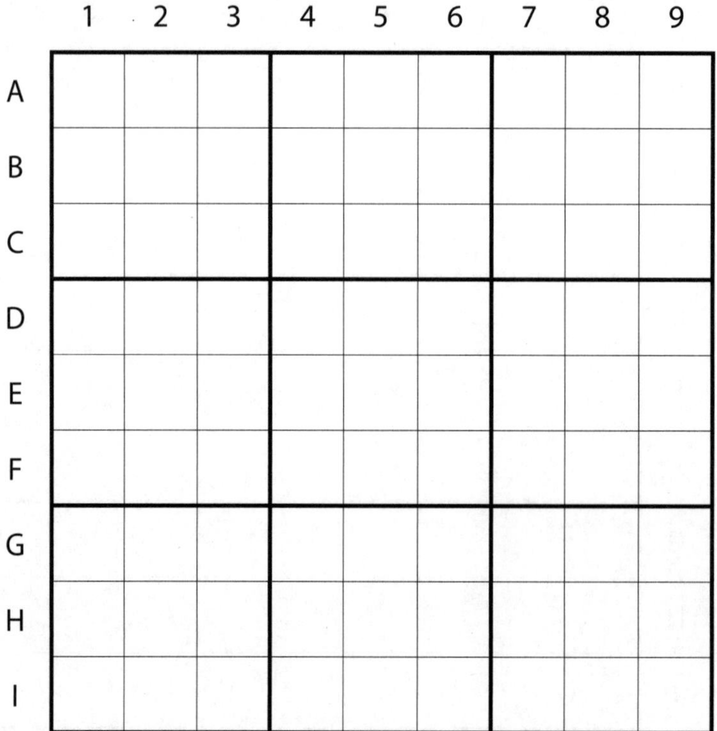

A1, G2, I9
Omri reigned in Tirzah for ______ years. (1 Kings 16:23)

A7, D6, G1, H5
How many different languages did the people speak when they first started building the Tower of Babel? (Gen. 11:1-9)

B2, D7, F1, G4
How many servants received talents in the parable of the talents? (Matt. 25:14-15)

B5, H9, I6
How many days after a baby boy's birth was Abraham told to circumcise him? (Gen. 17:12)

B6, D8, F5, G9, H3
Over how many days was the Festival of Unleavened Bread celebrated? (Exod. 12:14-17)

B7, C2, F4
How many unmarried daughters did Philip have? (Acts 21:8-9)

C3, D1, F8, I7
How many books in the Bible did Moses write?

D5, E2, G7, H6
Which verse in Luke 9 does Herod admit to beheading John?

E8, G5, I2
For the ______ plague (ordinal number), God sent frogs to cover the entire country. (Exod. 8:1-15)

6, 1, 3, 8, 7, 4, 5, 9, 2

1 = B3, C4, E9, F2, I8; 2 = A9, B1, C6, D4, F3, H7; 3 = A5, C9, E6, H8, I3; 4 = A6, D9, E3, G8, H1, I5; 5 = A4, B9, E5, G6, H2; 6 = B8, C5, D3, E7, F6, H4; 7 = A2, C7, E1, I4; 8 = A8, C1, D2, E4, F7, G3; 9 = A3, B4, C8, F9, I1

Challenge 58

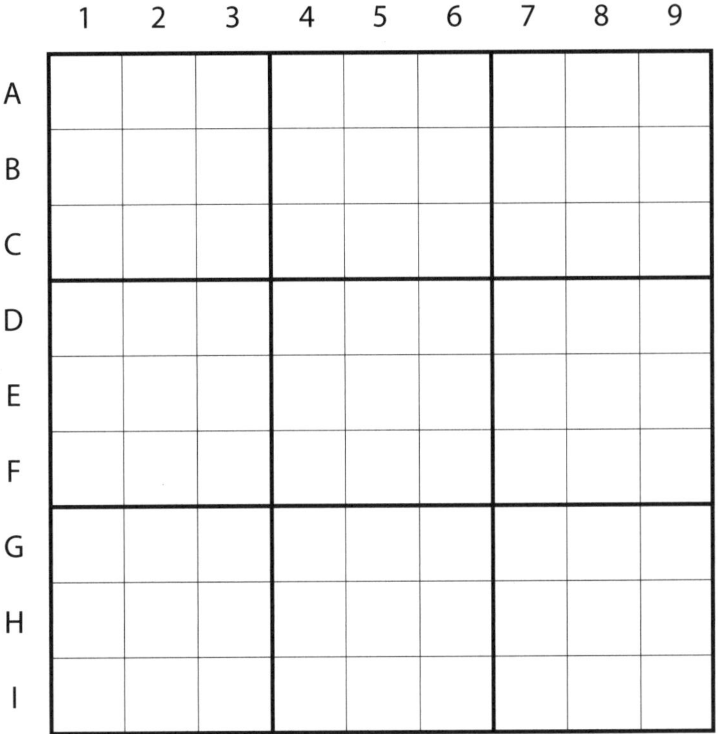

A2, E6, F7
How many years of famine did Joseph warn would come upon Egypt? (Gen. 41:30)

A6, H3, I4
How many living creatures did John see? (Rev. 4:6)

A7, D5, H1
How many towns did the descendants of Aaron receive from the tribes Judah and Simeon? (Josh. 21:13-16)

A8, B1, F2, H7
Divide the number of Jesus' disciples by two. (Matt. 10:1)

B3, E1, H4
The plague that riddled the Egyptian's livestock with disease was the ______ plague (ordinal number). (Exod. 9:1-7)

B6, C3, F1
How many years had Aeneas been bedridden when Peter found him? (Acts 9:33)

B9, G8, H2, I6
How many rams were to be sacrificed on the fifth day? (Num. 29:26)

C2, D3, F6, G5, H8
How many chapters are there in the Old Testament book Nahum?

C9, E2, F8, H6
How many sons did Esau have with his wife Adah? (Gen. 36:4)

7, 4, 9, 6, 5, 8, 2, 3, 1

1 = A3, B5, D4, G1, I7; 2 = A1, C5, D7, E3, F4; 3 = A4, B7, E9, I1; 4 = B8, C1, D2, E7, F5, G9; 5 = A5, C7, D6, F9, G2, I8; 6 = C4, D9, E5, G6, I3; 7 = B4, C8, D1, G3, H9, I5; 8 = A9, D8, E4, G7, H5, I2; 9 = B2, C6, E8, F3, G4, I9

MEDIUM

Challenge 59

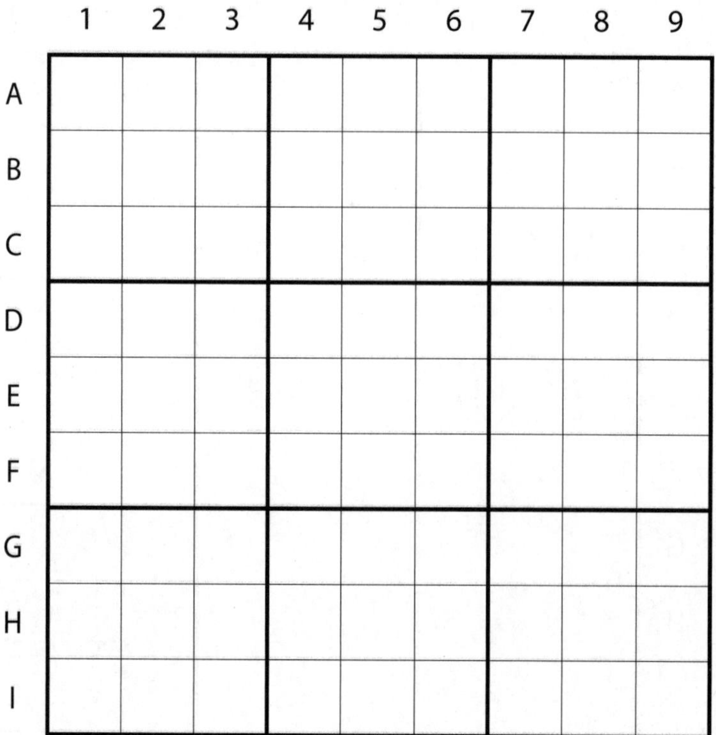

A3, D6, G4, I9
How many sheep did Nabal's wife, Abigail, give to David and his men? (1 Sam. 25:18-20)

A6, B2, G8, H5
Esau had ______ hundred men (ordinal number) with him when he met Jacob. (Gen. 33:1)

A8, D9, F4
Psalm 128 has ______ verses (amount).

B4, E8, G6
In the parable of the talents, how many talents (bags of silver or gold) did the man entrust to his servants in total? (Matt. 25:15)

B7, D1, G5
How many daughters-in-law did Noah have? (Gen. 7:13)

C5, D3, E9, I8
Take the number of days Jonah spent in the belly of the fish and multiply it by three. (Jonah 1:17)

C8, E4, F7, I1
How many messengers did John the Baptist send to Jesus? (Luke 7:18)

D8, E5, G1
How many scrolls are mentioned in Revelation 5:1?

E2, H9, I4
How many times did Naaman have to bathe in the Jordan River to cure his leprosy? (2 Kings 5:10)

5, 4, 6, 8, 3, 9, 2, 1, 7

1 = A2, B9, C4, F3, H7, I6; 2 = A5, B3, D2, G9, H6; 3 = A4, C3, E6, F9, H8, I2; 4 = C9, D4, E7, F1, I3; 5 = B5, C7, E1, F8, H2;
6 = B6, C2, E3, G7, H1, I5; 7 = A1, B8, C6, D7, F5, G3; 8 = A9, C1, D5, F2, H3, I7; 9 = A7, B1, F6, G2, H4

Challenge 60

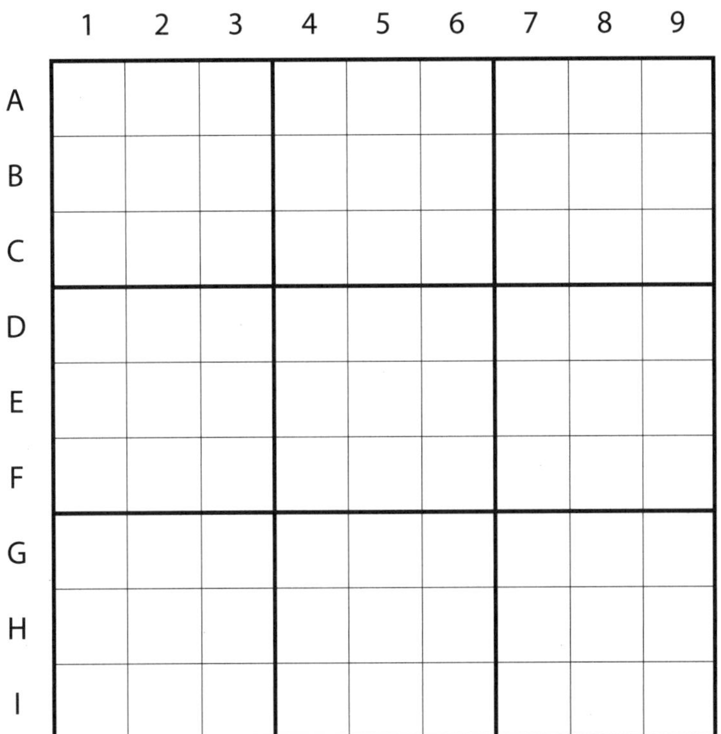

MEDIUM

A4, F9, I7
How many churches in Asia did John write a letter to in Revelation? (Rev. 1:4)

A7, C5, F6, I1
On which day did God separate the waters from the sky? (Gen. 1:6-8)

A9, C1, H5
The number of Jesus' disciples minus 9.

B2, F3, I5
How many sons did Jesse, David's father, have? (1 Sam. 16:10-12)

B5, C9, D7, E2
The Lord blessed Job with ______ thousand camels. (Job 42:12)

B6, D8, E5, G2
Psalm 100 has ______ verses (amount).

C2, D3, H1
In which of the first 10 chapters of Genesis, in verse 14, does the rainbow appear in the sky?

D4, F2, G3
How many chapters are there in the New Testament book of Philemon?

D5, G8, H3
How many chapters are there in the New Testament book Philippians?

7, 2, 3, 8, 6, 5, 9, 1, 4

1 = A5, B1, C8, E7, H6, I9; 2 = B3, D2, E8, G9, H4; 3 = B4, D6, E3, F8, G7, I2; 4 = A2, B9, C4, E1, F7, I6; 5 = A3, C7, F1, H9, I4;
6 = A1, F4, G6, H8, I3; 7 = B8, C3, D1, E6, G5, H2; 8 = A8, C6, D9, E4, G1, H7; 9 = A6, B7, E9, F5, G4, I8

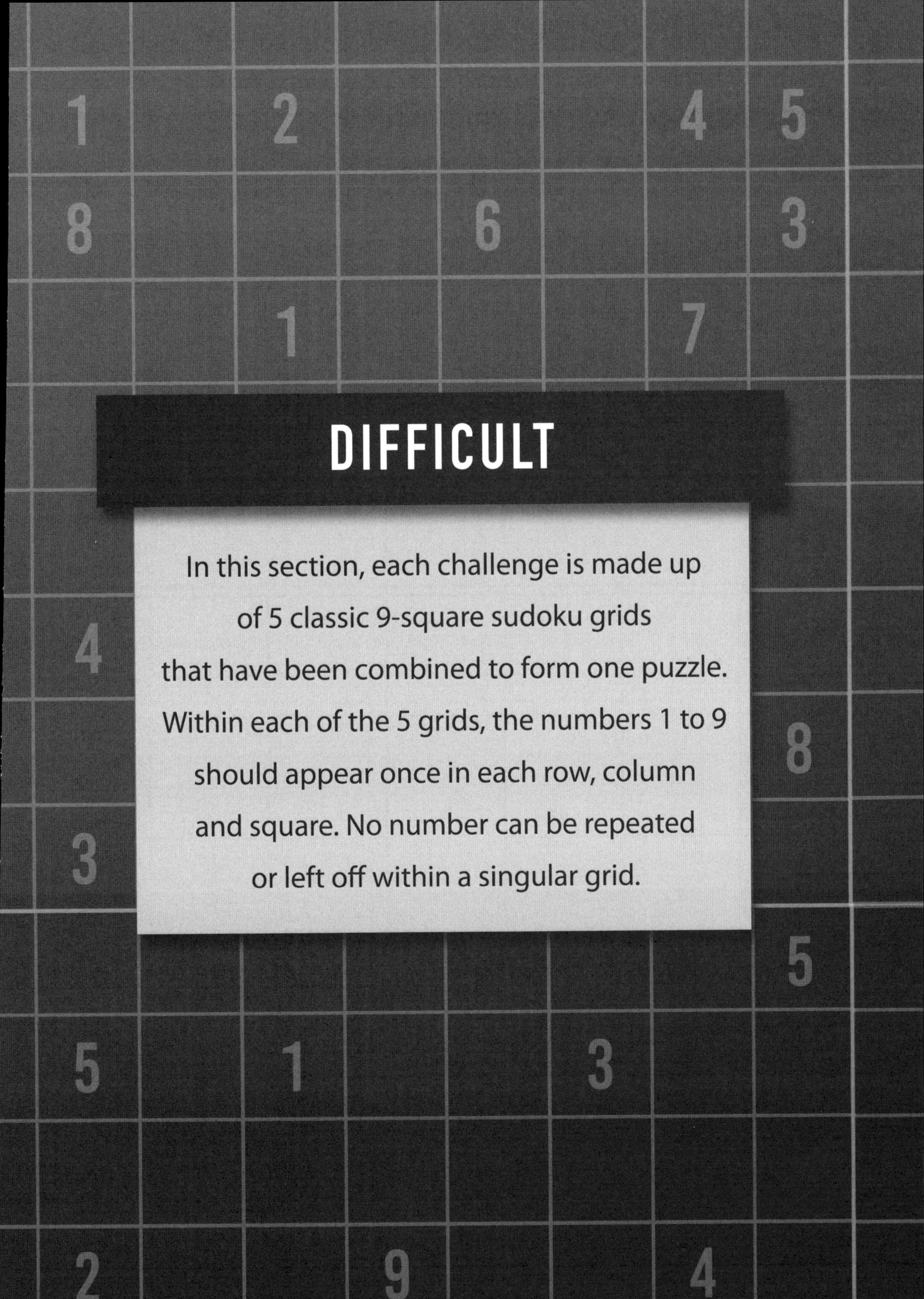

DIFFICULT

In this section, each challenge is made up of 5 classic 9-square sudoku grids that have been combined to form one puzzle. Within each of the 5 grids, the numbers 1 to 9 should appear once in each row, column and square. No number can be repeated or left off within a singular grid.

Challenge 61

			8				3	7				6				8		4	5	
5	8			7										9	7	6				
	3			4	6		8					8	2		3			1		9
				2			6					9	5		4		6			
	9	7			4								6		2		8	5	9	
		4	1			7		2						4		9			7	
1	4				2				4	9				5		2	9	7		
	5		7				4					2	9		8	4				
					3	2	5		1	3		4	7						2	6
						9			8	6		7	4							
						4	6		2					9						
								2	9				1	3						
		6			7					4		5	2							3
		1	3				2		3	1				4	8			1	2	
7					8		9		7	2		3				4			6	
		9			6	2						6				9	8		1	
5		3		2	1		7					8		3	1					6
			8				4	1									6	5		8
9		4			3	8							3	2	5			8		4
2		7		8			1	3								8		2	3	
			1		2			9					9	8	3					7

Challenge 62

	3				2		9						9	8				6		
	6						5	8						7		2	6		5	
9				5									4		1			7		9
		5			7			9					8				5		9	
2	4				8	7	3							5	8		3	2		7
		1	9									1			6		2		4	8
		3			5	1			7			8		9			4	1		
	5						8			1	2					6				2
	1			8	9		7				8		3	1				4		5
							5	8	4			2		6						
											5									
						2	1			6	9		4	8						
6		9	1		4				1		6	4	8			7				9
2						8		9	2						3		9	8	2	
					8					8				3	2	8		7	5	
4		6	2		1	5		3				7	2			5			9	
7		3			5	9		2				8				3		2		
				4			7						3				8		4	7
9		4	7		2	3							1							
	2		4		3		1								6				8	3
		7						4				5				4			7	

Challenge 63

	7	6					9	2
		1		9			6	
8								
	3			4			2	
	5		8					
9	8		3		6	1		5
7				5				
		5	9			7		6
2								

	1	6	2			9		7
				9				
3					4		5	
6				5	2		7	
				3		4		
	3	9	1			5		8
1			5		8	7		
	2					6		
		3		6				5

				3	5	1		
7		6					2	
				6				3
8				9	3			2
		2	5					
5			2			6	4	
		8	1		6			7
1		5					8	

9	4		5	7				8
3					9	1		5
	9		1					3
		5		8			4	
2					6	7		
	6			1			3	2
			2					
8					4	5		

		7	1			8		6
	8				4	5		
	4	9		2		3		8
								9
6		8			7		1	
	7		2			6		3
				6				
8					9		5	

Challenge 64

		9			1		3					9				1				
1				7											7		9	4		
		2			8	7		5					2		5					9
	8		7		2	3									1		2		8	5
		7			5		2					5		6		3		9		
2				3				7									5		4	
4		8			7	2				8	1			5	6				3	
		1	3					8	5				6				8		9	
				9							6			2				7		
									2			7								
							2							8						
								5		7	3	6								
	8					6					8				3				2	
		5		6				2		4				3		2		4		1
		3		8					3	1		2								
	1			5	8							3		4			9	2		
			9				7							7		3		9		
4			2				9	8												7
3					1	7		5					1			8	3	6		
		4	6									4			5	7				9
5				2		9							6					3		

DIFFICULT

Challenge 65

7				2		6		8							5	7				
8					9								2	9				8		4
	9	2				4		5								8			1	
	1				6								1		3				8	
6			5			9						6					1			
			7					6						3	8					1
2					3			9	4			1					7	9		3
5		6	9			8					1		7		4				2	
4					8			7				9	3		2		8			
								1	5	3										
								6			8		5							
						7	5		2		6			8						
		4	9				7		3		9			5	2				3	7
8	9		7		2			5				2					4			
					5				1	5			4	3	8	5			1	
	2				6	7							2			9		8	4	
	5		8	7			2	4							1		2		9	
1				3				6				3	7			4				1
9			6				1								9		1	3		
		8		2		5	6					4	1				3			9
7				5				9						7	4					6

Challenge 66

	9				3	8		4				9				7			4	8
					9								8			2				
7		4		1			5					5								
	1	9			5	7							1	6	5	3			9	
			8					9					3							1
4			9	2			6					8				1	2	7		
	2					4				9	3	1		2	7				8	
		5			4		9		8							9				6
	4		1									4	9				1	3		5
								2		8										
									3		6		4							
							6							1						
		7			4			6		5		7				1				
4				8									2				7	1		6
		8				9			2	3					5					
	7		9				8						7	3		8		9		
				6		3														1
2		6			1			5				6			2		5		4	
7					9			8					4			6		5		
				2		1								9						8
	6		3	1			4					1					2		3	

DIFFICULT

Challenge 67

	5						2						3	4		1		2		5
				7																7
9					3			1				9					6			
5		3		1		9		2					4		1	9				2
					5											8		9		
	4		7				6					7		9		6	5			
			1			2												5		6
7	9			5				4	7		3		6			3	4			
		8					3						9							
										1				8						
							4					5								
											2			6						
7				9				5	8						3				5	
							2				6				5				7	
2				4			7		9			6		1			2			
	3		9			6		4					2				8		1	
				7													6	9		
1		2					8					5		6		7				3
3		8		1								2				4		5		1
					3		9							3						
	2		6		4			7					6		9		7		8	

Challenge 68

<table>
<tr><td></td><td>8</td><td></td><td>7</td><td></td><td>1</td><td>6</td><td></td><td>4</td><td></td><td></td><td></td><td></td><td></td><td>1</td><td>4</td><td></td><td>2</td><td>9</td><td>6</td><td></td></tr>
<tr><td></td><td></td><td>7</td><td></td><td></td><td></td><td></td><td></td><td></td><td></td><td></td><td></td><td></td><td></td><td></td><td>3</td><td></td><td></td><td></td><td></td><td></td></tr>
<tr><td>9</td><td></td><td></td><td></td><td>2</td><td></td><td></td><td>3</td><td></td><td></td><td></td><td></td><td>5</td><td>4</td><td></td><td></td><td>7</td><td></td><td></td><td>3</td><td>8</td></tr>
<tr><td></td><td></td><td>2</td><td></td><td></td><td></td><td></td><td>6</td><td>9</td><td></td><td></td><td></td><td></td><td>1</td><td>8</td><td>2</td><td></td><td>5</td><td>7</td><td>9</td><td></td></tr>
<tr><td>1</td><td></td><td></td><td></td><td>6</td><td></td><td></td><td>8</td><td></td><td></td><td></td><td></td><td></td><td></td><td></td><td></td><td></td><td></td><td>5</td><td></td><td></td></tr>
<tr><td></td><td>4</td><td></td><td></td><td>8</td><td>5</td><td></td><td></td><td></td><td></td><td></td><td></td><td>4</td><td></td><td></td><td></td><td>6</td><td></td><td></td><td></td><td>3</td></tr>
<tr><td></td><td>2</td><td>8</td><td></td><td></td><td>3</td><td></td><td>4</td><td></td><td>5</td><td>2</td><td></td><td>1</td><td>8</td><td></td><td></td><td></td><td>4</td><td></td><td>7</td><td></td></tr>
<tr><td>7</td><td></td><td></td><td>6</td><td></td><td></td><td></td><td></td><td></td><td></td><td></td><td>3</td><td></td><td>7</td><td></td><td>8</td><td>1</td><td></td><td></td><td>5</td><td></td></tr>
<tr><td>4</td><td></td><td></td><td></td><td></td><td>2</td><td>3</td><td></td><td>1</td><td></td><td>9</td><td></td><td>2</td><td></td><td></td><td></td><td></td><td>6</td><td></td><td></td><td>1</td></tr>
<tr><td></td><td></td><td></td><td></td><td></td><td></td><td>5</td><td></td><td></td><td></td><td>8</td><td></td><td>6</td><td></td><td></td><td></td><td></td><td></td><td></td><td></td><td></td></tr>
<tr><td></td><td></td><td></td><td></td><td></td><td></td><td></td><td>9</td><td></td><td>6</td><td></td><td></td><td></td><td></td><td>7</td><td></td><td></td><td></td><td></td><td></td><td></td></tr>
<tr><td></td><td></td><td></td><td></td><td></td><td></td><td>8</td><td></td><td>4</td><td></td><td>7</td><td>2</td><td>3</td><td></td><td></td><td></td><td></td><td></td><td></td><td></td><td></td></tr>
<tr><td>8</td><td></td><td>2</td><td></td><td></td><td></td><td></td><td>1</td><td>9</td><td>2</td><td></td><td></td><td>4</td><td></td><td>8</td><td></td><td></td><td>7</td><td></td><td></td><td>5</td></tr>
<tr><td></td><td></td><td></td><td>2</td><td>8</td><td></td><td></td><td></td><td>5</td><td></td><td></td><td>8</td><td>7</td><td></td><td>2</td><td>9</td><td></td><td></td><td>6</td><td></td><td></td></tr>
<tr><td>3</td><td>4</td><td></td><td></td><td>1</td><td></td><td></td><td>8</td><td>2</td><td></td><td></td><td>1</td><td></td><td></td><td></td><td></td><td></td><td>4</td><td>1</td><td></td><td>7</td></tr>
<tr><td></td><td>2</td><td>8</td><td>3</td><td></td><td></td><td></td><td></td><td>1</td><td></td><td></td><td></td><td></td><td>8</td><td></td><td>7</td><td>2</td><td></td><td>9</td><td></td><td></td></tr>
<tr><td></td><td></td><td></td><td></td><td></td><td>2</td><td>5</td><td></td><td></td><td></td><td></td><td></td><td></td><td></td><td></td><td>5</td><td></td><td></td><td></td><td>4</td><td></td></tr>
<tr><td>4</td><td>5</td><td></td><td></td><td>7</td><td>9</td><td></td><td>6</td><td></td><td></td><td></td><td></td><td>3</td><td></td><td>5</td><td>4</td><td></td><td>6</td><td></td><td></td><td>1</td></tr>
<tr><td></td><td>8</td><td></td><td>4</td><td></td><td>3</td><td>1</td><td></td><td>7</td><td></td><td></td><td></td><td>8</td><td></td><td>6</td><td></td><td></td><td>2</td><td></td><td></td><td>9</td></tr>
<tr><td></td><td></td><td></td><td></td><td></td><td></td><td></td><td></td><td>4</td><td></td><td></td><td></td><td></td><td></td><td>1</td><td>3</td><td></td><td></td><td></td><td>6</td><td></td></tr>
<tr><td>5</td><td></td><td>4</td><td>7</td><td>9</td><td></td><td></td><td>2</td><td></td><td></td><td></td><td></td><td></td><td>5</td><td></td><td></td><td>4</td><td></td><td>7</td><td>1</td><td></td></tr>
</table>

DIFFICULT

Challenge 69

	9	3	2		1			6				8	3		1			4	5	
					8	9											9	6		
	8			5			7					2		6		8				7
	5			2	7	4							9	7	6				4	
2														2				7		
6		8	9				2	1				5				3				1
9	3		7		2	6			2		5		7	3		6	1	5		4
				8			9						2		8					
8	6				3			7	6		9			5	7			1		
						7	4		5		6									
								8		2			6							
								6		4	7	5								
		8	6	1			5		7				3	9					4	2
2			7		9									7			6	9		
3	6					8	7			5	3	2				1				8
	9		3	6		5						3		1		5		2		4
		5		7												4				
1		6		5	4	7		8					6		9	3			7	
	8		1		6		4	5				9			8	7				6
5								6												
6		3		2		9							2	4			3	5	8	

Challenge 70

	4	7	3		8	1							8	3		6		1		2
								3												
2		3		6			9	7				5			3		7		4	
	9				2	6		1					7	8	6			5		1
		1	4															7		
3				5			7					2				7	3		9	
4		9	2		3	5	1		4		9	8		7	4		6		1	
		6						2				6	9						8	
8			6		5	7			8		3				7	3				4
								7	3		4			1						
								8					5							
						1	6		5	9		7	4							
7			4	3	9		2			4		3			1				8	
		4		2		6		1			5	4		2		3			1	5
2					6		3			7			1	6	8		2		7	
	7		9			2							3		5			8	4	
		9						6						8			7			
5		8		1			4					6		1		2		7		9
	1		3		4			2				7			6				2	
					5	1							2		9					
	5			6			9							5	2		4		9	

Challenge 71

1	2		3		8	5		7						4	5			7		6
			7					4					1			7				
9		7		6			1					9	7			8		1	3	
			8		1	9		5				8			3		1		7	9
	1				9									3						2
7	9			4			3						6			4		5		3
	4				3	7		9			1		2				5			7
8		1	9	5					8			5		1		9			4	8
5				2				1	5		2					2			5	
						8		5					6	9						
						6		2		5		1								
								7		8				3						
3	7				4			8	1						2		8	1		6
		2				5				2	8	3		6	5					
4				2		1	7	3					4	2		1		7	9	
1		7			5			2				7			8		4		1	3
		6				9						1					7			
	4			6		7							2					5		
		3		4		8						5				8				
	2		1				5						3			9		8		
9	5		2		6		1								1	3		9		7

Challenge 72

9		6				4		7				3	8				4	1	7	
		3		4		6							2			1		8		
	1		8											6	9					5
8		9		5		7		1				8	9			5	2		1	
2					1			8					5			6		9		
	4		6		8		3								3			5		4
		8		2						2		9			2		5		6	
	5					8	9		3		1		4				6		9	
			9		6			3		8				1		3				
							3		1				8							
								2		9		1								
						6	8					2	9							
	6		2		8				8		6	4		9		8		6	5	
		4			7	9		5			3		1		5		6			4
7	1				5		2		7	1			5			4	9		1	
		6	8	2		1						2		4				3		5
	8						5							8			3			
3			5		9			4					6		9		4		7	
	9		4				3					9		2		7		5		6
2								6				7				6				
1		7		5	6	8		2				6	3		4				8	

DIFFICULT

Challenge 73

	3		9	5			7					4		1		7				9
																	5			
4				6	2	1		8					6				1		8	
3		8		4	9	2		7					4	3			8	6	9	
								9							9					
	5		6		7		1					5				1			7	
		3	4		5	7	2		5		9		1	4		8			5	
6	2			3		9				1		8			5		9	4		3
				7	6		8	1					5					7		
						6	9			5			8							
						2		7	8			5		6						
										9			7							
	5		2				7	9		3	8		6			9				7
7					5				4			9		8	4		2			1
6				7		5		8		6		7	4					8	3	
		3	6					7					5		8		9		2	
	9				8	2								9						
1				4	9							4		7			1	9		3
	3		1		6	7						5		6			3	4		2
		4						1												
2		1	4	9			8	5					7		1	5			9	

Challenge 74

1		2	3	6			5						9			5	3		7	
	4				8	9		3					2		8			5		4
8		1	6				4	5					8	6	3			1		7
				4											7					
	7				2	3						2		7			9		5	
	1				6			4			1		6				4	7		
3		9	4			1			6			4			2				8	
			8	2		6			8				7		9			3		5
								3			4			6						
						2						3								
								6	3				9	1						
9		2	1	6			8	5		7	6	2		3	5			7		
					3	7										6			1	
6		1		8		3				1	8	6		7		2			5	
	2				1	5		8						2			9	6	7	
			9										8		7				3	
7		6	8	4			3					4			3	1				5
	9	3	7		6	8							2		9		5	4		
								7						5						
1				5			2					7				3	1			8

DIFFICULT

Challenge 75

1		3		8				4					5	8		1		4		7
		7		3		8									7					
	5					3	2					9		7			3		2	
2		1		9	5			6				5		3	2		1		4	9
				1															5	
	8	9				1	3						7			8		6		
	1		9			6				9	2		3		1			9		4
7		6		2				8			4	6		1		9				
			4				1						9	4	5				6	1
							5			7			1							
									2											
						3		6		8	1	4	5							
	3	7			4	8		1			9		7			4		8		
4			6	8			3		8			2		9	6	8		7		
1								4	3			1					5		2	
	7	5		4		1							3		2	9		6		
		4																		
6			8	5		4		2				8		1	5		7		4	2
7		3				6		8				3		7	4		9		6	8
					8												6			
8			5		7		4	9				6	1			5		2	9	

Challenge 76

	6		8		7	2						7		1		8	2			
								3						8		5		1		
5		9	3	1			4						6					8		4
	1	6	7		4	5		2				3		7		2	4	9		
						1													3	
9				3			8						5		1					8
6		1	4				2	5	4					3		4		6		9
				2	9			1			5		2				5		1	
		5				8	7			3		5		6		3		4		
							8			1				5						
								2				7		9						
							5	9		2			8							
8				7		2			8	4		5		7			2	8		
			4		1	5						4	1		5		7	2		
7		9		6			4	8			7				1					9
	4		7		9		6						7			2			4	
	3					9						8				7				
5				2	3			1				2		6			1	5		7
		1	5		7	6									2	6			8	1
							5						8						2	
9		5	2	3				4					2	3			4			

DIFFICULT

Challenge 77

7		4	5				2	8
9				2				
	3					6	9	
		7	9		5			2
	5				8	4		
3				1	4		6	
4		1			9		8	
	9				2			1
				4				

	5				2	1	3	
		2						
8		1		7	4	2		9
	4		2				1	
3		8		5	7	9		6
	7		9					
						5		4
		3	7				9	

	8				9		7	
		1						
			2	7				3
	6		9	1		3	4	
			4					9
4					7	8		
	3				1			8
1		4	8			6		
	9				3		1	

5		8	7				3	
		6		8		1		4
4			3				9	
	5		4				2	
		3				7		
1				3	6	9		8
9			1		7		6	3
	1	4	6	2		5		

		8		3	6			
6			4				9	
	1			5		3		2
		5	3		2			1
2							8	
	7				8			
	8			2		4		
		6						9
1		7			5		3	6

Challenge 78

8		4		5			2					5		9	6		3		7	4
								9												
	6		3		7	1							2			1		8		
	8		6		5	2		7				8		5	3					7
					8														2	
9				3	2		4						6			4	1	9		
1		8		6			7			1		9						7		
7	3				4				3		8					5				
				7			1					6		2	1		4	5		8
						6		7	5			3								
						8					6		1							
								1	8	3				6						
		1		7			3						9			4	2		1	
4	3									8	2									
			3		4	1		6	9			2		7	3		1		8	5
	6		9			3									2			3		1
		3		8									3			5		7		
7					2			1				4	7				6		9	
	1			9		4							8			2		1		
			1				7													4
5			2		3			8				7		4			3		5	

Challenge 79

	9				6	7		2							4	5		7		8
		1	2					4						8	1					
8				5			3					2					6		3	
	5	9	6		3	8						9		3	2				7	6
																			5	
2				4		3	1						4			8	7			
9		5		6		2		8	6				3			2		6		
			8					5			2	8				3				5
7				9			6		8				2				8			9
						3	5		1					6						
										6		7								
						7			9		4									
1				3	8		2		4			5				8			6	
						5		9	7			3		4			6	9		1
2		7	9				3			9						9			3	
	1	5			3	2							1	5	4			2		
			6												6					5
7			5	9			4	8				7		6			9		8	
5	9			8			6					1		9	8				2	7
												4								
	7	2	1		9	4		3								5	1	3		

Challenge 80

8		9	1	2				5				9					6		4	
				3				1												
3					6	4							5	8		7		2		1
9				1			5					2		9	6		5		7	4
		4	7																5	
	3				8	2							8			3		1	2	
		8	2		1		7		6				9	2	5			4		
4							6			2						9	1			5
					9			2	3			8	6		7					
							8		7		1									
						2								8						
								5		8		6								
			1			4				7			5		4		7		2	6
9		3				8		7	9			2		6				8		
					7			9			6				6					1
	7		9				6						1	9		4		6		2
		1		2										2						
4				5	8	1		3				8		7	2		3		5	
5		7			1			2						5	8		4		6	3
																	1			
	4		8	7		9	3						7			2		9		

DIFFICULT

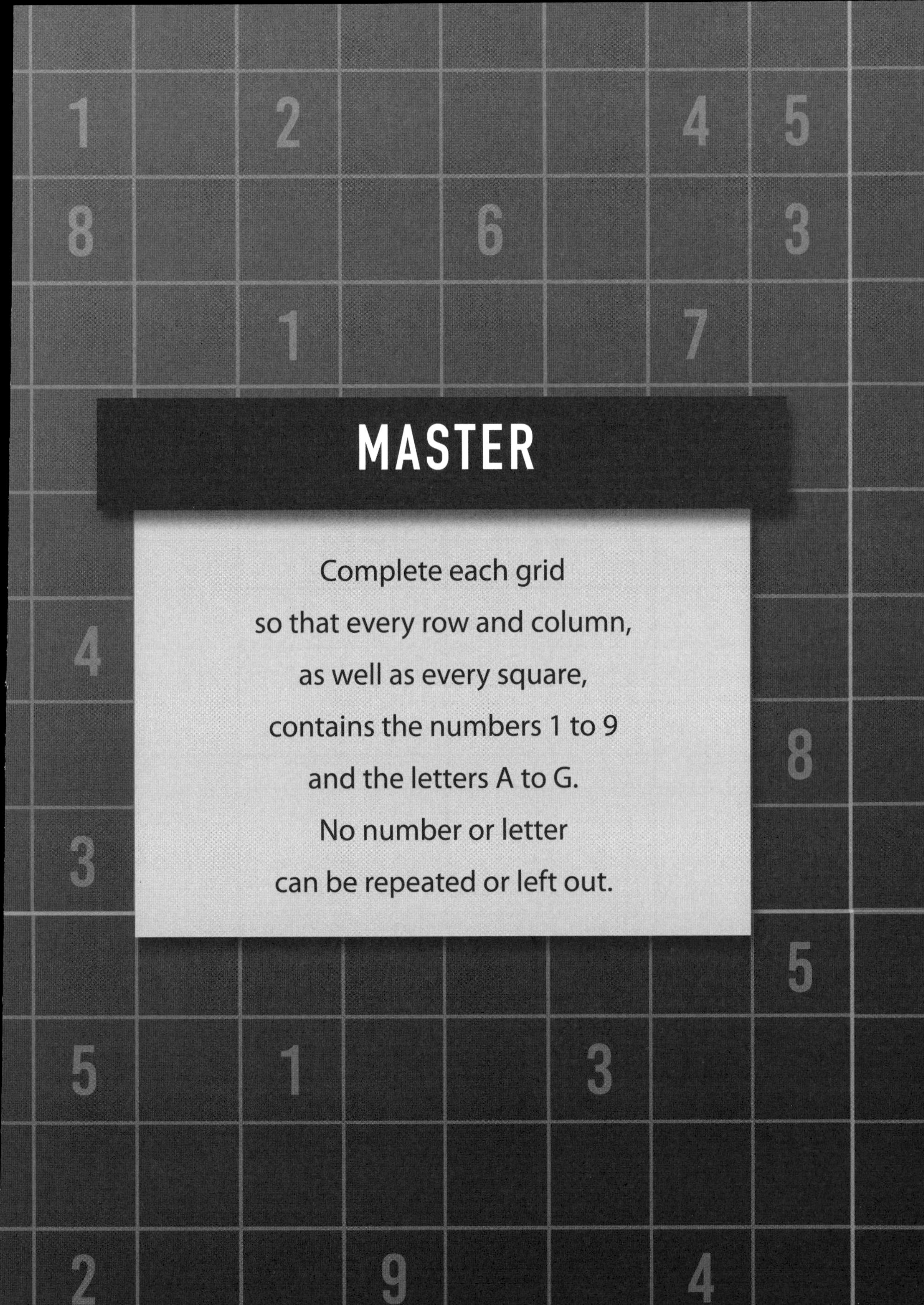
MASTER
Complete each grid
so that every row and column,
as well as every square,
contains the numbers 1 to 9
and the letters A to G.
No number or letter
can be repeated or left out.

Challenge 81

G		7	1	B			5	A					9	6	
8						1	7	G		6		5			3
9		C					E		5		F	7			B
			6	3	G		C	9		D		E	8		
3		1	G		B		D	2	6				F		7
		4		E				B		9		1	3		5
2	7				3	G					5		B		E
			9	7				3		G		6		A	C
C		A	3	D		2		7		B	1			F	4
5			2		7		8						C		
	4			6		F		5		3		8		2	
		8	F		E				A	2	6		5		
		3		A		C		4		5	9			7	
4		B				7		D			G		1		
	8				D					C				E	G
D			5	G		E					8	3			A

Challenge 82

4	1	F		3			D			5	6		8		G
	D						5			A		1			
			B		7	9			G		8			E	4
9		8					1	E		D	3		6		
D		2		4		3		6		C			9		8
		E				6	B		7			2			
	6		C	9			2	F						A	
	8		9		A					4	1		C		6
2		1		D	3				5			8	7		A
E			3		6	B				8			2		
B	C						9	G			2			4	
7		A		5					D		E		B		
			1		4			5		B		9	A		7
	E	4		B		5		A		7					2
			5		C						4		D	3	
8			A			1	F		3					6	

Challenge 83

5			A	8	4			1	C		F	B	E		2
	G		8		F	1		2			B	9			3
	2	F	6		B				D	A					
D		B	E			2	5	3		8	4	F		C	
8	9			G	D			F		C			2	B	A
A	4			1			F	B		7		5	3		
6		1	C			E			A						8
E					5		B		8		G		1		6
		A		4		7		C	1		6	E		2	
G		8	4		6		1	5		B			9		
		6			E		2		3		A	8		G	
2	7		F			5	3	D			8	6			
9			3	D		4				1	C	2	7		B
4		D			1	F			B				5		
		C		7	3					2	5	1			4
B		7				9	E	A		3	D		C		F

Challenge 84

E		2			A			G		3		F			1
			6			4	3			8			E		
	7		4	B					C	E	9			D	
8			F		2		E				D	4	3		G
9			E	A		5			3		G		B		6
			5		6				8		1	E			F
7	G						B			9				A	
		F		2	C		9	6		D		5	7		
2			9			D			7			B	1		E
				6			G	E	B	1				F	
G			7							2		D	A		
1		8	B		E	9	2	5			C				3
	E		2	5	D				G			1			
	5			3				B	2		8			E	
4		7				2	F			C			6		
F			1	8			C	D	A			2			7

MASTER

Challenge 85

	9		6	4		D		G		C	E		8		5
	D					G		5							9
2		7			E				3		A	1		B	
F				6			3	9	B			7	C	2	
6		9	3			4	7		C				5		8
	A		B		2	C		7		F		3			
						8	A	1		B	5				
		5		9		6	E		4		D		G	1	C
	3	6		1		B		2		7	C				F
		4			C						8	6			B
G			7				5		9				1	D	
5	F		E			3	9	B					7		2
		3		B	D				7		2	5			E
1		B					4		E				3		
						E		4			3		B		
E			5	3		A				D					7

Challenge 86

1	8		E	6		2				3			A		9
	2					C		9		A			E		8
		7		A	4						B	F			
D		4		E			1	8	G		F	7	3	5	
	B		1		G	6				5		D			A
			G	2				4			C			B	
	7						4	B							
A	4		D		1	E			6			5			3
8			B	F			2		C	7			4		
2					3		C		9					8	
	5	3				D		1			E				G
			4	B				G		F		3			5
		1		G							5	9			
		G	2		C					9	D		1		4
	3					B	A	E						6	
7	A		9		8		E	6		2				3	F

MASTER

Challenge 87

8				6		B	G	7	E		2	D	C	1	
	B		G			2	7	C	1		D	3	9	A	
			7		4		C	9	A	5			G	6	8
4		1			5		9	G	6	8			7	E	F
	9	5	3	G	B		8	2	F		7	4		D	C
		8	B		2		F	D	4			5		3	
E			2		D			3		A				B	
1	C		D	9	3	A		B		6	G		E	2	7
9	5		A		G	8	6	F	7		E	1	4	C	
G	8				7	F		4	C				5	9	
	F			D		4		5					8		B
	4	D	1	3		5	A	8		B	6	E	F		2
3			5	8			B		2		F		D	4	
B							2		D				3		
2	E				1		D	A	3				B		6
D	1		4	5	A		3	6	B		8		2	F	E

Challenge 88

	6		B			E	8	G		1		C		3	
		A		3	7			5		B				G	
D					B		F				8		4		2
8	C		7			9			E		2	6			F
4			3	9			1	E	2			F		6	B
	2			C		F			8			D			
B			5		3	8				G			A		4
		9		E				6		5	B			C	7
	4		E	2	9				B	6		7		8	
G		2	9		E		A	8		C					
		F			C					9	G		E		A
3	7		C	F			5		4		A	1			G
9			D			3		B			6				E
		4		B			6		3		C	G			9
	3			4			E							7	
6	5		F				9			2	E	3	8		C

Challenge 89

8		G	4	C	B			2			9	D			6
		C		3		A	8		4					E	
D	6			G					A		1	8	C		F
			A	2		E	D	C			8			4	B
A			3		9	G			2	D			B		8
	8		C				E			9		A		3	
E				B	8		5		3		A				9
		F	G	6			A	B		8	5		7	2	D
	G	E				9		5				6		1	C
F			9	A	G					C			5		3
6			1	E			B	A		G		7		D	
	C	A			2		7	4			6	F			
3		1			E	7				4	G				5
			7		4			1					D	6	
2				9		B				A					E
	5	8			A		3	D			2	G			4

Challenge 90

A			E	4			5	C		6	3		B	8	
8		2	7	9	A				4		F	6			C
F		C				7	2	1		E		D			5
			D		8		C				A		9	F	1
E	1				6		G	B				A	5	D	
		G	A		7		B	4		8			1		9
7						F			C		E	3		6	
D	2	4		5		A	9	G			6		C		
	F	D		3		G		7			2		A	1	
C	A			8		9	E	D	3		5			2	
			9		2			E		G		4			6
2	8		B	F			7		A	9		G	3		
	D		5	7		2		3		C		1			A
	7		2				3		E		9	5		4	F
	E			D	9		F	8					6		3
9		3	C		4		A		D		B	2			

MASTER

Challenge 91

D	7				E	4		8			2	B	G		9
5		4	E			6				1				D	
C	F		2		B			9		D			6		7
		6	B		3	G		7	A	5		2			
3	A		9			C		6			F	8	D		
		D	7		F	5	2	G	C	B			1		A
			8		9					3				E	4
	G	1		A			3	4		E			C		6
9					4			C			6	G	3		1
7			6		A	E	F	5	2	8		4	B		
			4	1	G		8			9	A			7	5
8	5	B		D		3	9			7				F	
A	3		D		5	7		2			C		8		B
		7		2			6	E		G	1	C	9	A	
	2		C					3	F		D				
	E		1		C	9		B		4		D			2

Challenge 92

B			C	A	8					F	E	1		6	
		F			5		9			3	C		D		G
7	4					3	C	B				A			
		2		7	4		E	1	D	6				3	C
5			A	4		E			6			8		C	B
	6			D		C		8		G	A	5	F		
		E							3					G	A
D			B	8		G	A	5			7	4			1
	9		D	F		7			C		8			A	
	C		8			1		2	G		5			7	
2				3	C	B									D
F		7					5	6	9		D	3	C		8
			F		1					5		C	B		3
G	A			E		4	F	C			3		1	D	
		8	3	G	B		2	9			6		A		F
9					A	8			1			G	7		2

MASTER

Challenge 93

D	8		3			5		G				2	1	6	
							A		D	8	3				E
	6			8	9				B			D			7
2		1	E		C				6		A		G		3
6		2			D			F		B	1	8		7	
	E		1	7		9				6				3	
8		D			B		1	9		3		6	2	A	
	3		C	A		2			8						1
	C		2			6			7	G		A	B		9
A		B		C	4	3				E	9				
	5		9			8	2	B			D		4		F
7		8		1					3				6		D
	D	E				7	6		G		8	1			B
	F			9							B			D	4
G			B			A	4	3				5	F		
1		A	8	D				E		5		G			6

Challenge 94

A	4			D	8					3	C			1	
C		D	2			A					5	3			
				7			E		D			2		4	A
G		1	6		4				F		A	E			C
B			7		C		1				F				8
		E		6		F			2	1		D			
8				3			D		E				G	6	
	G		D		A			5				1		C	
D			A		6		G			C	7	5			9
7	3			B		9		F			D			E	
9			5		3					G			4		
1	6			4	E			3		5		A	2		
3		C		G			F		A		E	B		5	
E	9		B	A		6				4	2	F			3
		A					4			B			D	7	
2			8	5	7			9	1				C		E

MASTER

Challenge 95

	8	G	7				4	A	2		1		5		
D	4		A	E				3			5	2		B	
					F				D	4			C		A
	B		E	A			6				C			4	3
8			G	C			3				D	6			5
		9	1			D			4				F		G
6		F		G			A		7		9			3	1
4			5		8			G		E		B	2		
7		6				B		2		1	8	E	4		
		8		2			1		G					C	D
			2			6				5		7		1	
3	1		D	9			5				6	A			2
G		7				3	D	B	1	2		5		F	
			B	6				4		F		G			
		E	4	8		A				D		1			B
5	F				1				9		E			D	4

Challenge 96

	2		6	1		8	F	4			E				B
				D		3		6		A		5		8	
	3	D	B		G				5			C			
5			1		C		4		7	D			A		2
		8	5		9		C			3	B	A	2		
A	6			8			5	C							7
		3			D			G		8					5
D			7						1			9		4	C
2		6		F		5	1		4			B	3		D
8			9	B		7	D	A		6					1
									2		7	8		A	
3		B	D		2	G				F		E			9
6			G				8	E			9	7		D	3
F	1		8	C	4		E		B		D		G		
		C				D					A	F			
B	D		E	G	6		3	2		5	1		C		8

Challenge 97

8		F			7	D			E	A		1	5		9
			9		8		B	G			D		E		A
G			2			A		1			5			F	B
3	6		A	1	5		9		B	F			7		
	C	5				B		D	7			E	3		6
		G			E				5		1	F			
B						2	D			E				9	
A			6	5				8			4		D		1
D				A		6		9	1	5		8		B	F
6		A	5			1							2	G	
	9		E	B			5	2		G	F			6	7
4			F		D		7	A			E		9		5
5		9		8		F			G		2	A	6		3
	2		G				6				9	B			
7				3	2			5		1					C
E	A		3		9				4	8				7	D

Challenge 98

	E		4	3			7	6			D	C	9		G
9				C						8	7		A		
		7			2			5	3			E	6		D
1			D	E			4				G	3			7
5		E		G		B			D		9	4		6	
B	4				C		9				1	D		E	A
		9	C			6		E		5					
	G		1		5				4			7	2		9
4		A		5		G				7					F
	5				4					D		6		9	
D	6				1				2					3	
7			F		8		3	9			C	B			E
E					7		B	D			6	1		G	2
		B	7		G				1						6
	9				E		5			C		A		7	
C			2	A		F		7						4	5

Challenge 99

8	C					A	1		9	E		F		3	
9		D		3	6						G				B
			F	E						1		9		4	
7			2			9			A	3			5		8
C		G	4		A		3	5		D		7		B	
5				G		C			B		E			F	
			3		E		2			G		1	8	D	
B	7			1		5			6		3				9
4			9	B			E		3			8		5	1
	1				G		9		2	7					F
3		F				D		4				B	2		
		B		6		3	A		D		8		C		4
	4	9		8		1	5		E				F		3
	D		5				B			A			9		
F		3				G			1			E		2	7
	E		B	A			6	G	4		9				D

Challenge 100

G	3		B						C			8		2	D
		4	C		5	8	9	D			3			E	
	E					B		7			2	C			
9			8	1						6	E		F		5
		B	F	D		6	1					9	3		
3		8						A		1	4		E		
1	7			4					9			F		D	8
E			9		B		3	8		2	D		1		
D		6	2		G	1		9		4			5		F
	8	G					4		2		A	1			6
	A			B			5	G	3					C	
5	B		3		F	2	D				C		4		G
A	9		7		3	4		2			6		C		1
C		1		9			A			B	F		8		
	F				2			1	7			4		9	
8		2		G			C			A			B		3

MASTER

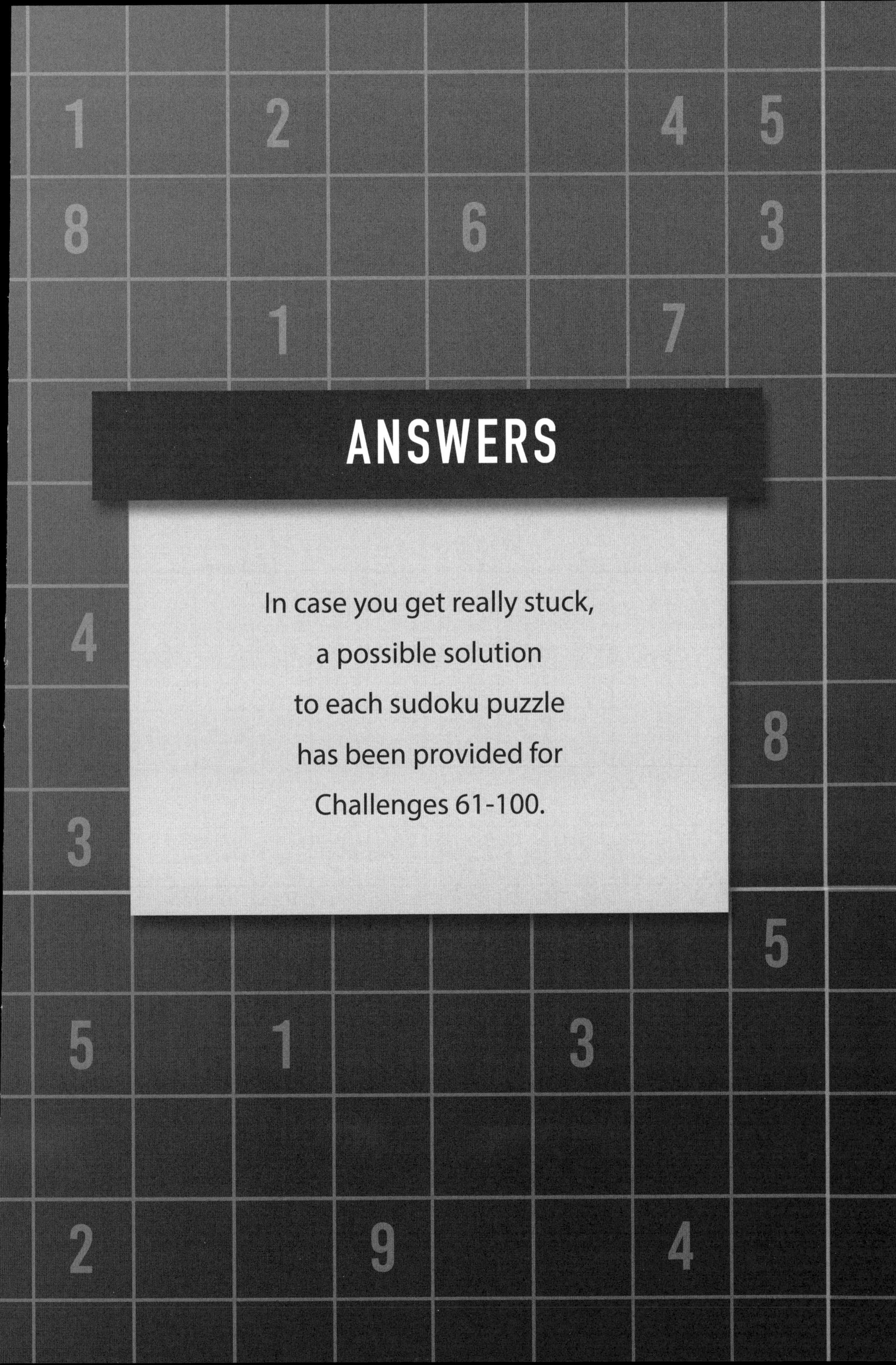

ANSWERS

In case you get really stuck,
a possible solution
to each sudoku puzzle
has been provided for
Challenges 61-100.

Challenge 61

4	2	1	8	5	9	6	3	7				6	1	3	9	8	2	4	5	7
5	8	6	3	7	1	9	2	4				5	4	9	7	6	1	2	8	3
7	3	9	2	4	6	1	8	5				8	2	7	3	5	4	1	6	9
3	1	5	9	2	7	4	6	8				9	5	2	4	7	6	8	3	1
2	9	7	6	8	4	5	1	3				7	6	1	2	3	8	5	9	4
8	6	4	1	3	5	7	9	2				3	8	4	1	9	5	6	7	2
1	4	3	5	9	2	8	7	6	4	9	2	1	3	5	6	2	9	7	4	8
9	5	2	7	6	8	3	4	1	5	8	7	2	9	6	8	4	7	3	1	5
6	7	8	4	1	3	2	5	9	1	3	6	4	7	8	5	1	3	9	2	6
						9	1	5	8	6	3	7	4	2						
						4	6	3	2	7	1	8	5	9						
						7	8	2	9	5	4	6	1	3						
4	2	6	9	5	7	1	3	8	6	4	9	5	2	7	6	1	9	4	8	3
8	9	1	3	6	4	5	2	7	3	1	8	9	6	4	8	7	3	1	2	5
7	3	5	2	1	8	6	9	4	7	2	5	3	8	1	2	4	5	7	6	9
1	4	9	7	3	6	2	8	5				6	4	5	7	9	8	3	1	2
5	8	3	4	2	1	9	7	6				8	7	3	1	5	2	9	4	6
6	7	2	8	9	5	3	4	1				2	1	9	4	3	6	5	7	8
9	1	4	6	7	3	8	5	2				7	3	2	5	6	1	8	9	4
2	6	7	5	8	9	4	1	3				4	5	6	9	8	7	2	3	1
3	5	8	1	4	2	7	6	9				1	9	8	3	2	4	6	5	7

Challenge 62

5	3	8	7	1	2	6	9	4				5	9	8	4	3	7	6	2	1
1	6	7	4	9	3	2	5	8				3	1	7	9	2	6	8	5	4
9	2	4	8	5	6	3	1	7				2	4	6	1	5	8	7	3	9
3	8	5	1	2	7	4	6	9				4	8	2	7	1	5	3	9	6
2	4	9	5	6	8	7	3	1				9	6	5	8	4	3	2	1	7
6	7	1	9	3	4	8	2	5				1	7	3	6	9	2	5	4	8
8	9	3	2	7	5	1	4	6	7	5	3	8	2	9	5	7	4	1	6	3
7	5	2	6	4	1	9	8	3	6	1	2	7	5	4	3	6	1	9	8	2
4	1	6	3	8	9	5	7	2	9	4	8	6	3	1	2	8	9	4	7	5
						3	5	8	4	7	1	2	9	6						
						6	9	4	8	2	5	3	1	7						
						2	1	7	3	6	9	5	4	8						
6	8	9	1	2	4	7	3	5	1	9	6	4	8	2	5	7	1	6	3	9
2	4	1	5	3	7	8	6	9	2	3	4	1	7	5	3	6	9	8	2	4
3	7	5	9	6	8	4	2	1	5	8	7	9	6	3	2	8	4	7	5	1
4	9	6	2	7	1	5	8	3				7	2	4	1	5	6	3	9	8
7	1	3	6	8	5	9	4	2				8	5	9	4	3	7	2	1	6
8	5	2	3	4	9	1	7	6				6	3	1	9	2	8	5	4	7
9	6	4	7	1	2	3	5	8				3	1	8	7	9	2	4	6	5
5	2	8	4	9	3	6	1	7				2	4	7	6	1	5	9	8	3
1	3	7	8	5	6	2	9	4				5	9	6	8	4	3	1	7	2

Challenge 63

5	7	6	4	1	8	3	9	2				5	1	6	2	8	3	9	4	7
3	2	1	7	9	5	8	6	4				4	8	7	6	9	5	1	3	2
8	4	9	2	6	3	5	1	7				3	9	2	7	1	4	8	5	6
1	3	7	5	4	9	6	2	8				6	4	8	9	5	2	3	7	1
6	5	2	8	7	1	9	4	3				7	5	1	8	3	6	4	2	9
9	8	4	3	2	6	1	7	5				2	3	9	1	4	7	5	6	8
7	6	3	1	5	4	2	8	9	7	3	5	1	6	4	5	2	8	7	9	3
4	1	5	9	8	2	7	3	6	4	1	9	8	2	5	3	7	9	6	1	4
2	9	8	6	3	7	4	5	1	8	6	2	9	7	3	4	6	1	2	8	5
						8	4	7	6	9	3	5	1	2						
						6	9	2	5	4	1	7	3	8						
						5	1	3	2	7	8	6	4	9						
9	4	6	5	7	1	3	2	8	1	5	6	4	9	7	1	5	2	8	3	6
1	5	7	8	2	3	9	6	4	3	8	7	2	5	1	6	8	3	9	4	7
3	8	2	4	6	9	1	7	5	9	2	4	3	8	6	7	9	4	5	2	1
7	9	4	1	5	2	6	8	3				1	4	9	5	2	6	3	7	8
6	3	5	9	8	7	2	4	1				7	3	5	8	4	1	2	6	9
2	1	8	3	4	6	7	5	9				6	2	8	9	3	7	4	1	5
5	6	9	7	1	8	4	3	2				5	7	4	2	1	8	6	9	3
4	7	3	2	9	5	8	1	6				9	1	3	4	6	5	7	8	2
8	2	1	6	3	4	5	9	7				8	6	2	3	7	9	1	5	4

Challenge 64

8	7	9	5	6	1	4	3	2				9	7	4	2	1	6	8	5	3
1	4	5	2	7	3	6	8	9				3	5	1	7	8	9	4	2	6
3	6	2	9	4	8	7	1	5				6	2	8	5	4	3	1	7	9
5	8	4	7	1	2	3	9	6				7	4	9	1	6	2	3	8	5
9	3	7	6	8	5	1	2	4				5	8	6	4	3	7	9	1	2
2	1	6	4	3	9	8	5	7				2	1	3	8	9	5	6	4	7
4	9	8	1	5	7	2	6	3	7	8	1	4	9	5	6	7	1	2	3	8
7	5	1	3	2	6	9	4	8	5	3	2	1	6	7	3	2	8	5	9	4
6	2	3	8	9	4	5	7	1	4	9	6	8	3	2	9	5	4	7	6	1
						3	8	6	2	5	4	7	1	9						
						7	2	4	1	6	9	3	5	8						
						1	9	5	8	7	3	6	2	4						
2	8	1	5	4	9	6	3	7	9	2	8	5	4	1	3	9	7	8	2	6
9	4	5	3	6	7	8	1	2	6	4	5	9	7	3	6	2	8	4	5	1
7	6	3	1	8	2	4	5	9	3	1	7	2	8	6	1	5	4	7	9	3
6	1	9	7	5	8	3	2	4				3	5	4	7	6	9	2	1	8
8	5	2	9	3	4	1	7	6				1	2	7	8	3	5	9	6	4
4	3	7	2	1	6	5	9	8				6	9	8	4	1	2	5	3	7
3	2	8	4	9	1	7	6	5				7	1	5	9	8	3	6	4	2
1	9	4	6	7	5	2	8	3				4	3	2	5	7	6	1	8	9
5	7	6	8	2	3	9	4	1				8	6	9	2	4	1	3	7	5

Challenge 65

7	4	3	1	2	5	6	9	8				8	6	1	5	7	4	3	9	2
8	6	5	3	4	9	1	7	2				7	2	9	1	3	6	8	5	4
1	9	2	8	6	7	4	3	5				3	4	5	9	8	2	7	1	6
3	1	8	2	9	6	7	5	4				2	1	7	3	6	5	4	8	9
6	2	7	5	3	4	9	8	1				6	9	8	7	4	1	2	3	5
9	5	4	7	8	1	3	2	6				4	5	3	8	2	9	6	7	1
2	8	1	4	7	3	5	6	9	4	7	3	1	8	2	6	5	7	9	4	3
5	7	6	9	1	2	8	4	3	9	2	1	5	7	6	4	9	3	1	2	8
4	3	9	6	5	8	2	1	7	6	8	5	9	3	4	2	1	8	5	6	7
						9	8	1	5	3	4	6	2	7						
						3	2	6	7	1	8	4	5	9						
						7	5	4	2	9	6	3	1	8						
5	3	4	9	6	8	1	7	2	3	4	9	8	6	5	2	1	9	4	3	7
8	9	6	7	1	2	4	3	5	8	6	7	2	9	1	7	3	4	6	5	8
2	7	1	3	4	5	6	9	8	1	5	2	7	4	3	8	5	6	9	1	2
4	2	3	5	9	6	7	8	1				1	2	6	3	9	7	8	4	5
6	5	9	8	7	1	3	2	4				5	8	4	1	6	2	7	9	3
1	8	7	2	3	4	9	5	6				3	7	9	5	4	8	2	6	1
9	4	5	6	8	7	2	1	3				6	5	2	9	7	1	3	8	4
3	1	8	4	2	9	5	6	7				4	1	8	6	2	3	5	7	9
7	6	2	1	5	3	8	4	9				9	3	7	4	8	5	1	2	6

Challenge 67

1	5	6	8	4	9	7	2	3				6	3	4	7	1	8	2	9	5
3	2	4	5	7	1	6	8	9				8	5	1	3	2	9	4	6	7
9	8	7	2	6	3	4	5	1				9	7	2	5	4	6	1	8	3
5	7	3	6	1	8	9	4	2				5	4	8	1	9	3	6	7	2
2	6	1	4	9	5	3	7	8				3	1	6	2	8	7	9	5	4
8	4	9	7	3	2	1	6	5				7	2	9	4	6	5	8	3	1
6	3	5	1	8	4	2	9	7	1	6	5	4	8	3	9	7	1	5	2	6
7	9	2	3	5	6	8	1	4	7	9	3	2	6	5	8	3	4	7	1	9
4	1	8	9	2	7	5	3	6	2	4	8	1	9	7	6	5	2	3	4	8
						6	5	2	3	1	9	7	4	8						
						1	4	3	6	8	7	5	2	9						
						7	8	9	4	5	2	3	1	6						
7	8	3	1	9	2	4	6	5	8	3	1	9	7	2	3	8	4	1	5	6
6	5	4	8	3	7	9	2	1	5	7	6	8	3	4	5	6	1	2	7	9
2	1	9	5	4	6	3	7	8	9	2	4	6	5	1	7	9	2	4	3	8
5	3	7	9	2	8	6	1	4				3	2	9	4	5	8	6	1	7
8	9	6	4	7	1	2	5	3				7	1	8	2	3	6	9	4	5
1	4	2	3	6	5	7	8	9				5	4	6	1	7	9	8	2	3
3	6	8	7	1	9	5	4	2				2	8	7	6	4	3	5	9	1
4	7	1	2	5	3	8	9	6				1	9	3	8	2	5	7	6	4
9	2	5	6	8	4	1	3	7				4	6	5	9	1	7	3	8	2

Challenge 66

5	9	2	6	7	3	8	1	4				9	2	1	3	7	6	5	4	8
1	8	6	4	5	9	3	7	2				6	8	3	4	2	5	9	1	7
7	3	4	2	1	8	9	5	6				5	7	4	1	8	9	6	3	2
6	1	9	3	4	5	7	2	8				7	1	6	5	3	8	2	9	4
2	7	3	8	6	1	5	4	9				2	3	9	6	4	7	8	5	1
4	5	8	9	2	7	1	6	3				8	4	5	9	1	2	7	6	3
9	2	1	5	3	6	4	8	7	5	9	3	1	6	2	7	5	3	4	8	9
3	6	5	7	8	4	2	9	1	8	6	4	3	5	7	8	9	4	1	2	6
8	4	7	1	9	2	6	3	5	7	1	2	4	9	8	2	6	1	3	7	5
						5	4	2	9	8	1	6	7	3						
						1	7	8	3	2	6	5	4	9						
						3	6	9	4	7	5	2	8	1						
3	1	7	5	9	4	8	2	6	1	5	9	7	3	4	6	1	8	2	9	5
4	5	9	2	8	6	7	1	3	6	4	8	9	2	5	4	3	7	1	8	6
6	2	8	1	7	3	9	5	4	2	3	7	8	1	6	5	2	9	3	7	4
5	7	3	9	4	2	6	8	1				5	7	3	1	8	4	9	6	2
1	8	4	7	6	5	3	9	2				4	8	2	3	9	6	7	5	1
2	9	6	8	3	1	4	7	5				6	9	1	2	7	5	8	4	3
7	4	1	6	5	9	2	3	8				2	4	7	8	6	3	5	1	9
8	3	5	4	2	7	1	6	9				3	6	9	7	5	1	4	2	8
9	6	2	3	1	8	5	4	7				1	5	8	9	4	2	6	3	7

Challenge 68

3	8	5	7	9	1	6	2	4				7	3	1	4	8	2	9	6	5
2	6	7	4	3	8	1	9	5				8	6	2	3	5	9	1	4	7
9	1	4	5	2	6	8	3	7				5	4	9	6	7	1	2	3	8
8	7	2	3	1	4	5	6	9				6	1	8	2	3	5	7	9	4
1	5	9	2	6	7	4	8	3				3	2	7	9	4	8	5	1	6
6	4	3	9	8	5	7	1	2				4	9	5	1	6	7	8	2	3
5	2	8	1	7	3	9	4	6	5	2	7	1	8	3	5	2	4	6	7	9
7	3	1	6	4	9	2	5	8	4	1	3	9	7	6	8	1	3	4	5	2
4	9	6	8	5	2	3	7	1	8	9	6	2	5	4	7	9	6	3	8	1
						5	2	7	3	8	9	6	4	1						
						1	9	3	6	5	4	8	2	7						
						8	6	4	1	7	2	3	9	5						
8	6	2	5	3	4	7	1	9	2	3	5	4	6	8	2	1	7	3	9	5
1	7	9	2	8	6	4	3	5	9	6	8	7	1	2	9	3	5	6	8	4
3	4	5	9	1	7	6	8	2	7	4	1	5	3	9	8	6	4	1	2	7
7	2	8	3	6	5	9	4	1				1	8	4	7	2	3	9	5	6
6	9	3	1	4	2	5	7	8				6	9	7	5	8	1	2	4	3
4	5	1	8	7	9	2	6	3				3	2	5	4	9	6	8	7	1
9	8	6	4	2	3	1	5	7				8	7	6	1	5	2	4	3	9
2	3	7	6	5	1	8	9	4				9	4	1	3	7	8	5	6	2
5	1	4	7	9	8	3	2	6				2	5	3	6	4	9	7	1	8

Challenge 69

7	9	3	2	4	1	8	5	6				8	3	9	1	7	6	4	5	2
5	1	6	3	7	8	9	4	2				7	1	4	5	2	9	6	3	8
4	8	2	6	5	9	1	7	3				2	5	6	3	8	4	9	1	7
3	5	1	8	2	7	4	6	9				1	9	7	6	5	2	8	4	3
2	4	9	1	6	5	7	3	8				3	4	2	9	1	8	7	6	5
6	7	8	9	3	4	5	2	1				5	6	8	4	3	7	2	9	1
9	3	5	7	1	2	6	8	4	2	1	5	9	7	3	2	6	1	5	8	4
1	2	7	4	8	6	3	9	5	8	7	4	6	2	1	8	4	5	3	7	9
8	6	4	5	9	3	2	1	7	6	3	9	4	8	5	7	9	3	1	2	6
						7	4	1	5	8	6	3	9	2						
						5	3	8	9	2	1	7	6	4						
						9	2	6	3	4	7	5	1	8						
9	7	8	6	1	3	4	5	2	7	6	8	1	3	9	5	8	7	6	4	2
2	5	4	7	8	9	1	6	3	4	9	2	8	5	7	4	2	6	9	3	1
3	6	1	5	4	2	8	7	9	1	5	3	2	4	6	3	1	9	7	5	8
4	9	7	3	6	8	5	2	1				3	7	1	6	5	8	2	9	4
8	3	5	2	7	1	6	9	4				5	9	2	7	4	1	8	6	3
1	2	6	9	5	4	7	3	8				4	6	8	9	3	2	1	7	5
7	8	2	1	9	6	3	4	5				9	1	5	8	7	4	3	2	6
5	1	9	4	3	7	2	8	6				6	8	3	2	9	5	4	1	7
6	4	3	8	2	5	9	1	7				7	2	4	1	6	3	5	8	9

Challenge 71

1	2	4	3	9	8	5	6	7				3	8	4	5	1	9	7	2	6
6	5	3	7	1	2	8	9	4				2	1	6	4	7	3	8	9	5
9	8	7	4	6	5	2	1	3				9	7	5	6	8	2	1	3	4
3	6	2	8	7	1	9	4	5				8	5	2	3	6	1	4	7	9
4	1	5	2	3	9	6	7	8				7	4	3	9	5	8	6	1	2
7	9	8	5	4	6	1	3	2				1	6	9	2	4	7	5	8	3
2	4	6	1	8	3	7	5	9	3	6	1	4	2	8	1	3	5	9	6	7
8	3	1	9	5	7	4	2	6	8	7	9	5	3	1	7	9	6	2	4	8
5	7	9	6	2	4	3	8	1	5	4	2	6	9	7	8	2	4	3	5	1
						8	4	5	2	1	3	7	6	9						
						6	3	2	9	5	7	1	8	4						
						9	1	7	4	8	6	2	5	3						
3	7	1	9	5	4	2	6	8	1	3	4	9	7	5	2	4	8	1	3	6
8	6	2	7	1	3	5	9	4	7	2	8	3	1	6	5	7	9	4	8	2
4	9	5	6	2	8	1	7	3	6	9	5	8	4	2	6	1	3	7	9	5
1	8	7	3	9	5	6	4	2				7	6	9	8	5	4	2	1	3
5	3	6	4	7	2	9	8	1				1	5	8	3	2	7	6	4	9
2	4	9	8	6	1	7	3	5				4	2	3	9	6	1	5	7	8
6	1	3	5	4	7	8	2	9				5	9	1	7	8	2	3	6	4
7	2	4	1	8	9	3	5	6				2	3	7	4	9	6	8	5	1
9	5	8	2	3	6	4	1	7				6	8	4	1	3	5	9	2	7

Challenge 70

6	4	7	3	9	8	1	2	5				4	8	3	9	6	5	1	7	2
9	8	5	7	2	1	4	6	3				7	1	9	2	8	4	6	5	3
2	1	3	5	6	4	8	9	7				5	6	2	3	1	7	8	4	9
5	9	4	8	7	2	6	3	1				9	7	8	6	4	2	5	3	1
7	2	1	4	3	6	9	5	8				3	4	1	8	5	9	7	2	6
3	6	8	1	5	9	2	7	4				2	5	6	1	7	3	4	9	8
4	7	9	2	8	3	5	1	6	4	2	9	8	3	7	4	9	6	2	1	5
1	5	6	9	4	7	3	8	2	7	5	1	6	9	4	5	2	1	3	8	7
8	3	2	6	1	5	7	4	9	8	6	3	1	2	5	7	3	8	9	6	4
						2	5	7	3	8	4	9	6	1						
						4	9	8	6	1	7	2	5	3						
						1	6	3	5	9	2	7	4	8						
7	6	1	4	3	9	8	2	5	1	4	6	3	7	9	1	5	6	2	8	4
3	9	4	5	2	8	6	7	1	9	3	5	4	8	2	7	3	9	6	1	5
2	8	5	1	7	6	9	3	4	2	7	8	5	1	6	8	4	2	9	7	3
4	7	6	9	5	3	2	1	8				2	3	7	5	9	1	8	4	6
1	2	9	8	4	7	3	5	6				9	5	8	4	6	7	1	3	2
5	3	8	6	1	2	7	4	9				6	4	1	3	2	8	7	5	9
9	1	7	3	8	4	5	6	2				7	9	4	6	1	3	5	2	8
6	4	2	7	9	5	1	8	3				1	2	3	9	8	5	4	6	7
8	5	3	2	6	1	4	9	7				8	6	5	2	7	4	3	9	1

Challenge 72

9	2	6	1	3	5	4	8	7				3	8	5	6	2	4	1	7	9
7	8	3	2	4	9	6	1	5				7	2	9	5	1	3	8	4	6
5	1	4	8	6	7	3	2	9				4	1	6	9	8	7	2	3	5
8	3	9	4	5	2	7	6	1				8	9	4	7	5	2	6	1	3
2	6	7	3	9	1	5	4	8				1	5	3	4	6	8	9	2	7
1	4	5	6	7	8	9	3	2				2	6	7	3	9	1	5	8	4
6	9	8	5	2	3	1	7	4	6	2	5	9	3	8	2	4	5	7	6	1
3	5	2	7	1	4	8	9	6	3	7	1	5	4	2	1	7	6	3	9	8
4	7	1	9	8	6	2	5	3	9	8	4	6	7	1	8	3	9	4	5	2
						5	3	9	1	6	2	7	8	4						
						7	4	2	5	9	8	1	6	3						
						6	8	1	4	3	7	2	9	5						
5	6	9	2	4	8	3	1	7	8	5	6	4	2	9	1	8	7	6	5	3
8	2	4	1	3	7	9	6	5	2	4	3	8	1	7	5	3	6	9	2	4
7	1	3	6	9	5	4	2	8	7	1	9	3	5	6	2	4	9	7	1	8
4	5	6	8	2	3	1	7	9				2	7	4	6	1	8	3	9	5
9	8	1	7	6	4	2	5	3				5	9	8	7	2	3	4	6	1
3	7	2	5	1	9	6	8	4				1	6	3	9	5	4	8	7	2
6	9	8	4	7	2	5	3	1				9	8	2	3	7	1	5	4	6
2	3	5	9	8	1	7	4	6				7	4	5	8	6	2	1	3	9
1	4	7	3	5	6	8	9	2				6	3	1	4	9	5	2	8	7

Challenge 73

2	3	1	9	5	8	6	7	4				4	8	1	6	7	2	5	3	9
8	9	6	7	1	4	5	3	2				9	3	2	8	4	5	1	6	7
4	7	5	3	6	2	1	9	8				7	6	5	3	9	1	2	8	4
3	6	8	1	4	9	2	5	7				2	4	3	7	5	8	6	9	1
7	1	4	5	2	3	8	6	9				1	7	6	9	2	3	8	4	5
9	5	2	6	8	7	4	1	3				5	9	8	4	1	6	3	7	2
1	8	3	4	9	5	7	2	6	5	8	9	3	1	4	2	8	7	9	5	6
6	2	7	8	3	1	9	4	5	3	1	6	8	2	7	5	6	9	4	1	3
5	4	9	2	7	6	3	8	1	7	2	4	6	5	9	1	3	4	7	2	8
						6	9	4	1	5	7	2	8	3						
						2	1	7	8	4	3	5	9	6						
						8	5	3	6	9	2	4	7	1						
3	5	8	2	6	1	4	7	9	2	3	8	1	6	5	3	9	8	2	4	7
7	4	9	8	3	5	1	6	2	4	7	5	9	3	8	4	7	2	5	6	1
6	1	2	9	7	4	5	3	8	9	6	1	7	4	2	6	1	5	8	3	9
4	8	3	6	5	2	9	1	7				3	5	1	8	4	9	7	2	6
5	9	6	7	1	8	2	4	3				6	2	9	5	3	7	1	8	4
1	2	7	3	4	9	8	5	6				4	8	7	2	6	1	9	5	3
9	3	5	1	8	6	7	2	4				5	9	6	7	8	3	4	1	2
8	6	4	5	2	7	3	9	1				8	1	4	9	2	6	3	7	5
2	7	1	4	9	3	6	8	5				2	7	3	1	5	4	6	9	8

Challenge 74

1	9	2	3	6	4	8	5	7				6	9	4	1	5	3	2	7	8
5	8	3	7	1	9	4	6	2				7	5	8	4	2	6	9	3	1
6	4	7	2	5	8	9	1	3				3	2	1	8	9	7	5	6	4
8	3	1	6	9	7	2	4	5				5	8	6	3	4	2	1	9	7
9	2	5	1	4	3	7	8	6				9	1	3	7	8	5	4	2	6
4	7	6	5	8	2	3	9	1				2	4	7	6	1	9	8	5	3
2	1	8	9	3	6	5	7	4	2	3	1	8	6	9	5	3	4	7	1	2
3	6	9	4	7	5	1	2	8	6	9	7	4	3	5	2	7	1	6	8	9
7	5	4	8	2	1	6	3	9	8	4	5	1	7	2	9	6	8	3	4	5
						9	1	3	7	8	4	5	2	6						
						2	5	7	1	6	9	3	8	4						
						8	4	6	3	5	2	7	9	1						
9	3	2	1	6	7	4	8	5	9	7	6	2	1	3	5	9	8	7	4	6
8	4	5	2	9	3	7	6	1	4	2	3	9	5	8	4	6	7	3	1	2
6	7	1	5	8	4	3	9	2	5	1	8	6	4	7	1	2	3	8	5	9
4	2	9	6	3	1	5	7	8				5	3	2	8	4	9	6	7	1
3	1	8	9	7	5	2	4	6				1	8	6	7	5	2	9	3	4
7	5	6	8	4	2	1	3	9				4	7	9	3	1	6	2	8	5
5	9	3	7	2	6	8	1	4				8	2	1	9	7	5	4	6	3
2	6	4	3	1	8	9	5	7				3	6	5	2	8	4	1	9	7
1	8	7	4	5	9	6	2	3				7	9	4	6	3	1	5	2	8

Challenge 75

1	6	3	2	8	9	7	5	4				2	5	8	6	1	9	4	3	7
9	2	7	5	3	4	8	6	1				3	4	6	7	5	2	1	9	8
4	5	8	6	7	1	3	2	9				9	1	7	8	4	3	5	2	6
2	7	1	3	9	5	4	8	6				5	6	3	2	7	1	8	4	9
5	3	4	8	1	6	9	7	2				1	8	9	3	6	4	7	5	2
6	8	9	7	4	2	1	3	5				4	7	2	9	8	5	6	1	3
3	1	2	9	5	8	6	4	7	1	9	2	8	3	5	1	2	6	9	7	4
7	4	6	1	2	3	5	9	8	7	3	4	6	2	1	4	9	7	3	8	5
8	9	5	4	6	7	2	1	3	5	6	8	7	9	4	5	3	8	2	6	1
						4	5	2	6	7	3	9	1	8						
						1	8	9	2	4	5	3	6	7						
						3	7	6	9	8	1	4	5	2						
5	3	7	2	9	4	8	6	1	4	2	9	5	7	3	9	4	2	8	1	6
4	2	9	6	8	1	7	3	5	8	1	6	2	4	9	6	8	1	7	5	3
1	6	8	3	7	5	9	2	4	3	5	7	1	8	6	3	7	5	4	2	9
2	7	5	9	4	6	1	8	3				4	3	5	2	9	8	6	7	1
3	8	4	7	1	2	5	9	6				7	6	2	1	3	4	9	8	5
6	9	1	8	5	3	4	7	2				8	9	1	5	6	7	3	4	2
7	4	3	1	2	9	6	5	8				3	2	7	4	1	9	5	6	8
9	5	6	4	3	8	2	1	7				9	5	8	7	2	6	1	3	4
8	1	2	5	6	7	3	4	9				6	1	4	8	5	3	2	9	7

Challenge 76

4	6	3	8	5	7	2	1	9				7	4	1	6	8	2	5	9	3
1	2	8	9	4	6	7	5	3				9	3	8	4	5	7	1	2	6
5	7	9	3	1	2	6	4	8				2	6	5	3	1	9	8	7	4
8	1	6	7	9	4	5	3	2				3	8	7	5	2	4	9	6	1
3	4	2	6	8	5	1	9	7				4	1	9	8	7	6	2	3	5
9	5	7	2	3	1	4	8	6				6	5	2	1	9	3	7	4	8
6	3	1	4	7	8	9	2	5	4	8	6	1	7	3	2	4	8	6	5	9
7	8	4	5	2	9	3	6	1	9	7	5	8	2	4	9	6	5	3	1	7
2	9	5	1	6	3	8	7	4	1	3	2	5	9	6	7	3	1	4	8	2
						6	8	3	7	1	9	2	4	5						
						4	1	2	6	5	8	7	3	9						
						7	5	9	3	2	4	6	8	1						
8	1	4	9	7	5	2	3	6	8	4	1	5	9	7	6	3	2	8	1	4
6	2	3	4	8	1	5	9	7	2	6	3	4	1	8	5	9	7	2	6	3
7	5	9	3	6	2	1	4	8	5	9	7	3	6	2	1	4	8	7	5	9
2	4	8	7	1	9	3	6	5				9	7	1	3	2	5	6	4	8
1	3	7	6	5	4	9	8	2				8	3	5	4	7	6	1	9	2
5	9	6	8	2	3	4	7	1				2	4	6	9	8	1	5	3	7
3	8	1	5	4	7	6	2	9				7	5	4	2	6	9	3	8	1
4	7	2	1	9	6	8	5	3				6	8	9	7	1	3	4	2	5
9	6	5	2	3	8	7	1	4				1	2	3	8	5	4	9	7	6

Challenge 77

7	6	4	5	9	3	1	2	8				9	5	4	6	8	2	1	3	7
9	1	8	4	2	6	3	7	5				7	3	2	5	9	1	4	6	8
2	3	5	8	7	1	6	9	4				8	6	1	3	7	4	2	5	9
6	4	7	9	3	5	8	1	2				5	4	9	2	6	8	7	1	3
1	5	2	7	6	8	4	3	9				6	1	7	4	3	9	8	2	5
3	8	9	2	1	4	5	6	7				3	2	8	1	5	7	9	4	6
4	7	1	6	5	9	2	8	3	1	6	9	4	7	5	9	2	6	3	8	1
5	9	6	3	8	2	7	4	1	3	5	8	2	9	6	8	1	3	5	7	4
8	2	3	1	4	7	9	5	6	2	7	4	1	8	3	7	4	5	6	9	2
						5	6	8	9	1	2	3	4	7						
						3	1	7	4	8	6	5	2	9						
						4	2	9	5	3	7	8	6	1						
5	9	8	7	1	4	6	3	2	7	4	1	9	5	8	2	3	6	1	7	4
2	3	6	9	8	5	1	7	4	8	9	5	6	3	2	4	1	7	5	9	8
4	7	1	3	6	2	8	9	5	6	2	3	7	1	4	8	5	9	3	6	2
6	5	9	4	7	8	3	2	1				8	6	5	3	7	2	9	4	1
8	4	3	2	9	1	7	5	6				2	9	1	5	6	4	7	8	3
1	2	7	5	3	6	9	4	8				4	7	3	1	9	8	6	2	5
9	8	2	1	5	7	4	6	3				3	8	9	6	2	1	4	5	7
7	6	5	8	4	3	2	1	9				5	4	6	7	8	3	2	1	9
3	1	4	6	2	9	5	8	7				1	2	7	9	4	5	8	3	6

Challenge 78

8	7	4	9	5	1	6	2	3				5	1	9	6	8	3	2	7	4
5	1	3	4	2	6	7	8	9				7	8	6	4	2	5	1	3	9
2	6	9	3	8	7	1	5	4				3	2	4	9	1	7	8	5	6
3	8	1	6	4	5	2	9	7				8	4	5	3	9	2	6	1	7
4	2	6	7	9	8	5	3	1				1	9	3	7	6	8	4	2	5
9	5	7	1	3	2	8	4	6				2	6	7	5	4	1	9	8	3
1	4	8	5	6	9	3	7	2	6	1	4	9	5	8	2	3	6	7	4	1
7	3	2	8	1	4	9	6	5	3	2	8	4	7	1	8	5	9	3	6	2
6	9	5	2	7	3	4	1	8	7	9	5	6	3	2	1	7	4	5	9	8
						6	2	7	5	4	1	3	8	9						
						8	9	3	2	7	6	5	1	4						
						5	4	1	8	3	9	7	2	6						
6	8	1	5	7	9	2	3	4	1	6	7	8	9	5	7	4	2	6	1	3
4	3	2	8	1	6	7	5	9	4	8	2	1	6	3	5	9	8	4	2	7
9	5	7	3	2	4	1	8	6	9	5	3	2	4	7	3	6	1	9	8	5
2	6	8	9	5	1	3	4	7				6	5	8	2	7	9	3	4	1
1	9	3	4	8	7	5	6	2				9	3	2	1	5	4	7	6	8
7	4	5	6	3	2	8	9	1				4	7	1	8	3	6	5	9	2
3	1	6	7	9	8	4	2	5				3	8	9	4	2	5	1	7	6
8	2	9	1	4	5	6	7	3				5	2	6	9	1	7	8	3	4
5	7	4	2	6	3	9	1	8				7	1	4	6	8	3	2	5	9

Challenge 79

3	9	4	1	8	6	7	5	2				6	9	1	4	5	3	7	2	8
5	7	1	2	3	9	6	8	4				3	5	8	1	7	2	9	6	4
8	6	2	4	5	7	9	3	1				2	7	4	8	9	6	5	3	1
1	5	9	6	2	3	8	4	7				9	8	3	2	1	5	4	7	6
4	3	7	9	1	8	5	2	6				7	1	2	6	4	9	8	5	3
2	8	6	7	4	5	3	1	9				5	4	6	3	8	7	1	9	2
9	4	5	3	6	1	2	7	8	6	4	5	1	3	9	5	2	4	6	8	7
6	1	3	8	7	2	4	9	5	3	1	2	8	6	7	9	3	1	2	4	5
7	2	8	5	9	4	1	6	3	8	7	9	4	2	5	7	6	8	3	1	9
						3	5	2	1	8	7	9	4	6						
						9	4	1	2	6	3	7	5	8						
						7	8	6	9	5	4	2	1	3						
1	5	9	4	3	8	6	2	7	4	3	8	5	9	1	4	8	3	7	6	2
3	8	4	7	2	6	5	1	9	7	2	6	3	8	4	2	7	6	9	5	1
2	6	7	9	1	5	8	3	4	5	9	1	6	7	2	1	9	5	8	3	4
4	1	5	8	7	3	2	9	6				8	1	5	3	4	7	2	9	6
9	2	8	6	4	1	3	7	5				9	2	3	6	1	8	4	7	5
7	3	6	5	9	2	1	4	8				7	4	6	5	2	9	1	8	3
5	9	3	2	8	4	7	6	1				1	3	9	8	6	4	5	2	7
6	4	1	3	5	7	9	8	2				4	5	7	9	3	2	6	1	8
8	7	2	1	6	9	4	5	3				2	6	8	7	5	1	3	4	9

Challenge 80

8	4	9	1	2	7	6	3	5				9	7	1	8	2	6	5	4	3
2	6	5	9	3	4	7	8	1				6	2	3	1	5	4	7	9	8
3	7	1	5	8	6	4	2	9				4	5	8	3	7	9	2	6	1
9	2	6	4	1	3	8	5	7				2	3	9	6	1	5	8	7	4
5	8	4	7	9	2	3	1	6				7	1	6	4	8	2	3	5	9
1	3	7	6	5	8	2	9	4				5	8	4	9	3	7	1	2	6
6	9	8	2	4	1	5	7	3	6	4	8	1	9	2	5	6	8	4	3	7
4	1	2	3	7	5	9	6	8	1	2	5	3	4	7	2	9	1	6	8	5
7	5	3	8	6	9	1	4	2	3	9	7	8	6	5	7	4	3	9	1	2
						6	8	4	7	3	1	5	2	9						
						2	3	1	5	6	9	4	7	8						
						7	9	5	4	8	2	6	1	3						
7	5	8	1	3	9	4	2	6	8	7	3	9	5	1	4	8	7	3	2	6
9	1	3	2	4	6	8	5	7	9	1	4	2	3	6	1	5	9	8	7	4
6	2	4	5	8	7	3	1	9	2	5	6	7	8	4	6	3	2	5	9	1
3	7	5	9	1	4	2	6	8				3	1	9	7	4	5	6	8	2
8	6	1	7	2	3	5	9	4				5	4	2	9	6	8	1	3	7
4	9	2	6	5	8	1	7	3				8	6	7	2	1	3	4	5	9
5	3	7	4	9	1	6	8	2				1	2	5	8	9	4	7	6	3
2	8	9	3	6	5	7	4	1				6	9	8	3	7	1	2	4	5
1	4	6	8	7	2	9	3	5				4	7	3	5	2	6	9	1	8

Challenge 81

G	F	7	1	B	8	D	5	A	E	4	3	C	9	6	2
8	B	E	D	F	9	1	7	G	C	6	2	5	A	4	3
9	3	C	4	2	A	6	E	8	5	1	F	7	G	D	B
A	2	5	6	3	G	4	C	9	7	D	B	E	8	1	F
3	E	1	G	5	B	9	D	2	6	A	C	4	F	8	7
F	C	4	8	E	2	A	6	B	D	9	7	1	3	G	5
2	7	6	A	C	3	G	1	F	4	8	5	D	B	9	E
B	5	D	9	7	F	8	4	3	1	G	E	6	2	A	C
C	6	A	3	D	5	2	9	7	8	B	1	G	E	F	4
5	D	9	2	1	7	B	8	E	G	F	4	A	C	3	6
E	4	G	B	6	C	F	A	5	9	3	D	8	7	2	1
7	1	8	F	4	E	3	G	C	A	2	6	9	5	B	D
6	G	3	E	A	1	C	2	4	B	5	9	F	D	7	8
4	A	B	C	8	6	7	F	D	3	E	G	2	1	5	9
1	8	2	7	9	D	5	3	6	F	C	A	B	4	E	G
D	9	F	5	G	4	E	B	1	2	7	8	3	6	C	A

Challenge 82

4	1	F	2	3	E	C	D	B	9	5	6	A	8	7	G
6	D	G	E	2	B	8	5	4	C	A	7	1	F	9	3
A	3	C	B	F	7	9	6	1	G	2	8	D	5	E	4
9	5	8	7	A	G	4	1	E	F	D	3	B	6	2	C
D	B	2	F	4	1	3	G	6	E	C	A	7	9	5	8
1	A	E	4	C	5	6	B	8	7	9	G	2	3	D	F
G	6	7	C	9	8	D	2	F	B	3	5	4	1	A	E
5	8	3	9	7	A	F	E	D	2	4	1	G	C	B	6
2	9	1	G	D	3	E	4	C	5	6	B	8	7	F	A
E	F	5	3	1	6	B	A	7	4	8	9	C	2	G	D
B	C	6	D	8	F	7	9	G	A	1	2	3	E	4	5
7	4	A	8	5	2	G	C	3	D	F	E	6	B	1	9
C	G	D	1	E	4	2	3	5	6	B	F	9	A	8	7
3	E	4	6	B	9	5	8	A	1	7	D	F	G	C	2
F	2	B	5	6	C	A	7	9	8	G	4	E	D	3	1
8	7	9	A	G	D	1	F	2	3	E	C	5	4	6	B

Challenge 83

5	3	9	A	8	4	G	D	1	C	6	F	B	E	7	2
7	G	4	8	C	F	1	6	2	5	E	B	9	D	A	3
C	2	F	6	E	B	3	7	G	D	A	9	4	8	5	1
D	1	B	E	9	A	2	5	3	7	8	4	F	6	C	G
8	9	3	5	G	D	6	4	F	E	C	1	7	2	B	A
A	4	G	D	1	C	8	F	B	6	7	2	5	3	9	E
6	B	1	C	2	7	E	9	4	A	5	3	D	G	F	8
E	F	2	7	3	5	A	B	9	8	D	G	C	1	4	6
3	5	A	B	4	8	7	G	C	1	9	6	E	F	2	D
G	C	8	4	F	6	D	1	5	2	B	E	A	9	3	7
1	D	6	9	B	E	C	2	7	3	F	A	8	4	G	5
2	7	E	F	A	9	5	3	D	G	4	8	6	B	1	C
9	6	5	3	D	G	4	A	8	F	1	C	2	7	E	B
4	A	D	2	6	1	F	C	E	B	G	7	3	5	8	9
F	E	C	G	7	3	B	8	6	9	2	5	1	A	D	4
B	8	7	1	5	2	9	E	A	4	3	D	G	C	6	F

Challenge 84

E	9	2	C	D	A	8	6	G	4	3	7	F	5	B	1
D	A	G	6	9	5	4	3	F	1	8	B	7	E	C	2
3	7	5	4	B	G	F	1	2	C	E	9	6	8	D	A
8	1	B	F	7	2	C	E	A	6	5	D	4	3	9	G
9	D	1	E	A	7	5	8	4	3	F	G	C	B	2	6
C	2	A	5	4	6	3	D	7	8	B	1	E	9	G	F
7	G	6	8	E	F	1	B	C	5	9	2	3	D	A	4
B	4	F	3	2	C	G	9	6	E	D	A	5	7	1	8
2	F	4	9	C	3	D	A	8	7	G	6	B	1	5	E
5	C	D	A	6	4	7	G	E	B	1	3	8	2	F	9
G	3	E	7	1	8	B	5	9	F	2	4	D	A	6	C
1	6	8	B	F	E	9	2	5	D	A	C	G	4	7	3
A	E	9	2	5	D	6	4	3	G	7	F	1	C	8	B
6	5	C	G	3	1	A	7	B	2	4	8	9	F	E	D
4	8	7	D	G	B	2	F	1	9	C	E	A	6	3	5
F	B	3	1	8	9	E	C	D	A	6	5	2	G	4	7

Challenge 85

B	9	1	6	4	7	D	2	G	F	C	E	A	8	3	5
3	D	A	4	C	1	G	B	5	2	8	7	E	6	F	9
2	5	7	C	8	E	9	F	D	3	6	A	1	4	B	G
F	G	E	8	6	A	5	3	9	B	1	4	7	C	2	D
6	1	9	3	D	B	4	7	E	C	2	G	F	5	A	8
4	A	G	B	5	2	C	1	7	8	F	9	3	D	E	6
C	E	D	F	G	3	8	A	1	6	B	5	2	9	7	4
8	7	5	2	9	F	6	E	3	4	A	D	B	G	1	C
9	3	6	A	1	4	B	D	2	G	7	C	8	E	5	F
D	2	4	1	E	C	7	G	F	5	3	8	6	A	9	B
G	B	C	7	2	8	F	5	A	9	E	6	4	1	D	3
5	F	8	E	A	6	3	9	B	D	4	1	C	7	G	2
A	4	3	G	B	D	1	C	8	7	9	2	5	F	6	E
1	6	B	9	7	G	2	4	C	E	5	F	D	3	8	A
7	8	2	D	F	5	E	6	4	A	G	3	9	B	C	1
E	C	F	5	3	9	A	8	6	1	D	B	G	2	4	7

Challenge 86

1	8	C	E	6	5	2	F	7	D	3	4	B	A	G	9
F	2	B	5	3	7	C	G	9	1	A	6	4	E	D	8
G	9	7	3	A	4	8	D	2	5	E	B	F	6	1	C
D	6	4	A	E	B	9	1	8	G	C	F	7	3	5	2
C	B	F	1	9	G	6	8	3	E	5	2	D	7	4	A
3	E	9	G	2	F	A	5	4	7	D	C	1	8	B	6
5	7	6	8	C	D	3	4	B	A	1	9	G	2	F	E
A	4	2	D	7	1	E	B	F	6	8	G	5	9	C	3
8	G	E	B	F	6	5	2	D	C	7	3	A	4	9	1
2	1	D	7	4	3	G	C	5	9	6	A	E	F	8	B
9	5	3	F	8	A	D	7	1	4	B	E	6	C	2	G
6	C	A	4	B	E	1	9	G	2	F	8	3	D	7	5
E	D	1	6	G	2	F	3	C	8	4	5	9	B	A	7
B	F	G	2	5	C	7	6	A	3	9	D	8	1	E	4
4	3	8	C	1	9	B	A	E	F	G	7	2	5	6	D
7	A	5	9	D	8	4	E	6	B	2	1	C	G	3	F

Challenge 87

8	3	A	9	6	F	B	G	7	E	4	2	D	C	1	5
5	B	6	G	E	8	2	7	C	1	F	D	3	9	A	4
F	2	E	7	1	4	D	C	9	A	5	3	B	G	6	8
4	D	1	C	A	5	3	9	G	6	8	B	2	7	E	F
6	9	5	3	G	B	1	8	2	F	E	7	4	A	D	C
A	7	8	B	C	2	E	F	D	4	1	9	5	6	3	G
E	G	4	2	7	D	6	5	3	8	A	C	F	1	B	9
1	C	F	D	9	3	A	4	B	5	6	G	8	E	2	7
9	5	B	A	2	G	8	6	F	7	3	E	1	4	C	D
G	8	2	6	B	7	F	E	4	C	D	1	A	5	9	3
C	F	3	E	D	9	4	1	5	G	2	A	6	8	7	B
7	4	D	1	3	C	5	A	8	9	B	6	E	F	G	2
3	6	G	5	8	E	7	B	1	2	C	F	9	D	4	A
B	A	7	8	F	6	9	2	E	D	G	4	C	3	5	1
2	E	C	F	4	1	G	D	A	3	9	5	7	B	8	6
D	1	9	4	5	A	C	3	6	B	7	8	G	2	F	E

Challenge 88

2	6	5	B	A	4	E	8	G	9	1	F	C	7	3	D
1	F	A	4	3	7	6	2	5	C	B	D	E	9	G	8
D	9	E	G	1	B	C	F	3	6	7	8	5	4	A	2
8	C	3	7	D	5	9	G	4	E	A	2	6	B	1	F
4	8	C	3	9	A	5	1	E	2	D	7	F	G	6	B
7	2	6	A	C	G	F	B	9	8	3	4	D	1	E	5
B	E	D	5	6	3	8	7	C	F	G	1	9	A	2	4
F	G	9	1	E	2	D	4	6	A	5	B	8	3	C	7
A	4	1	E	2	9	G	D	F	B	6	5	7	C	8	3
G	B	2	9	7	E	1	A	8	D	C	3	4	F	5	6
5	D	F	6	8	C	4	3	1	7	9	G	2	E	B	A
3	7	8	C	F	6	B	5	2	4	E	A	1	D	9	G
9	1	7	D	5	8	3	C	B	G	4	6	A	2	F	E
E	A	4	8	B	1	2	6	7	3	F	C	G	5	D	9
C	3	G	2	4	F	A	E	D	5	8	9	B	6	7	1
6	5	B	F	G	D	7	9	A	1	2	E	3	8	4	C

Challenge 89

8	7	G	4	C	B	5	1	2	E	F	9	D	3	A	6
9	B	C	5	3	F	A	8	G	4	6	D	1	2	E	7
D	6	2	E	G	7	4	9	3	A	B	1	8	C	5	F
1	F	3	A	2	6	E	D	C	5	7	8	G	9	4	B
A	1	6	3	7	9	G	C	E	2	D	4	5	B	F	8
5	8	B	C	4	D	2	E	F	G	9	7	A	6	3	1
E	D	7	2	B	8	F	5	6	3	1	A	4	G	C	9
4	9	F	G	6	1	3	A	B	C	8	5	E	7	2	D
7	G	E	8	F	3	9	4	5	D	2	B	6	A	1	C
F	2	4	9	A	G	D	6	7	1	C	E	B	5	8	3
6	3	5	1	E	C	8	B	A	9	G	F	7	4	D	2
B	C	A	D	5	2	1	7	4	8	3	6	F	E	9	G
3	A	1	6	D	E	7	2	9	F	4	G	C	8	B	5
G	E	9	7	8	4	C	F	1	B	5	3	2	D	6	A
2	4	D	F	9	5	B	G	8	6	A	C	3	1	7	E
C	5	8	B	1	A	6	3	D	7	E	2	9	F	G	4

Challenge 90

A	9	1	E	4	F	D	5	C	G	6	3	7	B	8	2
8	B	2	7	9	A	E	1	5	4	D	F	6	G	3	C
F	G	C	6	B	3	7	2	1	9	E	8	D	4	A	5
3	4	5	D	G	8	6	C	2	B	7	A	E	9	F	1
E	1	9	3	C	6	8	G	B	2	F	7	A	5	D	4
6	C	G	A	2	7	3	B	4	5	8	D	F	1	E	9
7	5	B	8	1	D	F	4	9	C	A	E	3	2	6	G
D	2	4	F	5	E	A	9	G	1	3	6	8	C	7	B
5	F	D	4	3	C	G	6	7	8	B	2	9	A	1	E
C	A	6	G	8	1	9	E	D	3	4	5	B	F	2	7
1	3	7	9	A	2	B	D	E	F	G	C	4	8	5	6
2	8	E	B	F	5	4	7	6	A	9	1	G	3	C	D
B	D	F	5	7	G	2	8	3	6	C	4	1	E	9	A
G	7	8	2	6	B	C	3	A	E	1	9	5	D	4	F
4	E	A	1	D	9	5	F	8	7	2	G	C	6	B	3
9	6	3	C	E	4	1	A	F	D	5	B	2	7	G	8

Challenge 91

D	7	A	3	F	E	4	5	8	6	C	2	B	G	1	9
5	9	4	E	7	2	6	C	F	G	1	B	3	A	D	8
C	F	G	2	8	B	A	1	9	4	D	3	E	6	5	7
1	8	6	B	9	3	G	D	7	A	5	E	2	4	C	F
3	A	5	9	E	1	C	4	6	7	2	F	8	D	B	G
E	4	D	7	6	F	5	2	G	C	B	8	9	1	3	A
2	6	C	8	B	9	D	G	A	1	3	5	F	7	E	4
B	G	1	F	A	7	8	3	4	D	E	9	5	C	2	6
9	D	E	A	5	4	2	7	C	B	F	6	G	3	8	1
7	1	3	6	C	A	E	F	5	2	8	G	4	B	9	D
F	C	2	4	1	G	B	8	D	3	9	A	6	E	7	5
8	5	B	G	D	6	3	9	1	E	7	4	A	2	F	C
A	3	F	D	G	5	7	E	2	9	6	C	1	8	4	B
4	B	7	5	2	D	F	6	E	8	G	1	C	9	A	3
G	2	9	C	4	8	1	B	3	F	A	D	7	5	6	E
6	E	8	1	3	C	9	A	B	5	4	7	D	F	G	2

Challenge 92

B	D	3	C	A	8	2	G	7	5	F	E	1	4	6	9
1	8	F	E	B	5	6	9	A	4	3	C	7	D	2	G
7	4	6	G	1	D	3	C	B	8	2	9	A	5	F	E
A	5	2	9	7	4	F	E	1	D	6	G	B	8	3	C
5	F	G	A	4	2	E	7	D	6	9	1	8	3	C	B
4	6	9	1	D	3	C	B	8	2	G	A	5	F	E	7
8	2	E	7	5	F	9	1	4	3	C	B	D	6	G	A
D	3	C	B	8	6	G	A	5	F	E	7	4	2	9	1
6	9	1	D	F	E	7	4	3	C	B	8	2	G	A	5
3	C	B	8	6	9	1	D	2	G	A	5	F	E	7	4
2	G	A	5	3	C	B	8	F	E	7	4	6	9	1	D
F	E	7	4	2	G	A	5	6	9	1	D	3	C	B	8
E	7	4	F	9	1	D	6	G	A	5	2	C	B	8	3
G	A	5	2	E	7	4	F	C	B	8	3	9	1	D	6
C	1	8	3	G	B	5	2	9	7	D	6	E	A	4	F
9	B	D	6	C	A	8	3	E	1	4	F	G	7	5	2

Challenge 93

D	8	C	3	B	F	5	E	G	9	4	7	2	1	6	A
9	4	5	7	6	2	G	A	1	D	8	3	F	C	B	E
F	6	G	A	8	9	1	3	2	B	C	E	D	5	4	7
2	B	1	E	4	C	D	7	5	6	F	A	9	G	8	3
6	A	2	G	3	D	4	C	F	E	B	1	8	9	7	5
4	E	F	1	7	8	9	5	C	A	6	2	B	D	3	G
8	7	D	5	E	B	F	1	9	4	3	G	6	2	A	C
B	3	9	C	A	6	2	G	D	8	7	5	4	E	F	1
3	C	4	2	5	E	6	D	8	7	G	F	A	B	1	9
A	1	B	D	C	4	3	F	6	5	E	9	7	8	G	2
E	5	6	9	G	7	8	2	B	1	A	D	3	4	C	F
7	G	8	F	1	A	B	9	4	3	2	C	E	6	5	D
C	D	E	4	F	5	7	6	A	G	9	8	1	3	2	B
5	F	3	6	9	G	E	8	7	2	1	B	C	A	D	4
G	9	7	B	2	1	A	4	3	C	D	6	5	F	E	8
1	2	A	8	D	3	C	B	E	F	5	4	G	7	9	6

Challenge 94

A	4	7	E	D	8	G	2	B	9	3	C	6	F	1	5
C	8	D	2	1	F	A	6	4	7	E	5	3	B	9	G
5	F	9	3	7	B	C	E	1	D	6	G	2	8	4	A
G	B	1	6	9	4	5	3	8	F	2	A	E	7	D	C
B	A	3	7	E	C	4	1	6	G	D	F	9	5	2	8
4	5	E	9	6	G	F	7	C	2	1	8	D	A	3	B
8	C	2	1	3	5	B	D	A	E	9	4	7	G	6	F
F	G	6	D	2	A	8	9	5	3	7	B	1	E	C	4
D	2	F	A	8	6	1	G	E	4	C	7	5	3	B	9
7	3	4	C	B	2	9	5	F	8	A	D	G	6	E	1
9	E	B	5	F	3	D	A	2	6	G	1	C	4	8	7
1	6	8	G	4	E	7	C	3	B	5	9	A	2	F	D
3	7	C	4	G	1	2	F	D	A	8	E	B	9	5	6
E	9	5	B	A	D	6	8	7	C	4	2	F	1	G	3
6	1	A	F	C	9	E	4	G	5	B	3	8	D	7	2
2	D	G	8	5	7	3	B	9	1	F	6	4	C	A	E

Challenge 95

9	8	G	7	D	3	C	4	A	2	B	1	F	5	6	E
D	4	C	A	E	9	1	8	3	F	6	5	2	G	B	7
2	6	1	3	7	F	5	B	E	D	4	G	9	C	8	A
F	B	5	E	A	2	G	6	7	8	9	C	D	1	4	3
8	7	2	G	C	4	F	3	1	B	A	D	6	9	E	5
B	A	9	1	5	6	D	E	C	4	3	2	8	F	7	G
6	E	F	C	G	B	2	A	5	7	8	9	4	D	3	1
4	D	3	5	1	8	9	7	G	6	E	F	B	2	A	C
7	G	6	9	3	D	B	C	2	A	1	8	E	4	5	F
A	5	8	F	2	E	4	1	9	G	7	B	3	6	C	D
E	C	B	2	F	A	6	G	D	3	5	4	7	8	1	9
3	1	4	D	9	7	8	5	F	E	C	6	A	B	G	2
G	9	7	8	4	C	3	D	B	1	2	A	5	E	F	6
1	3	D	B	6	5	E	9	4	C	F	7	G	A	2	8
C	2	E	4	8	G	A	F	6	5	D	3	1	7	9	B
5	F	A	6	B	1	7	2	8	9	G	E	C	3	D	4

Challenge 96

G	2	A	6	1	5	8	F	4	9	C	E	D	7	3	B
C	E	9	4	D	B	3	7	6	G	A	2	5	1	8	F
7	3	D	B	A	G	2	6	F	5	1	8	C	9	E	4
5	8	F	1	9	C	E	4	B	7	D	3	G	A	6	2
1	4	8	5	E	9	F	C	7	D	3	B	A	2	G	6
A	6	G	2	8	1	B	5	C	E	9	4	3	D	F	7
9	F	3	C	7	D	4	2	G	A	8	6	1	E	B	5
D	B	E	7	3	A	6	G	5	1	2	F	9	8	4	C
2	G	6	A	F	8	5	1	9	4	E	C	B	3	7	D
8	C	4	9	B	E	7	D	A	3	6	G	2	F	5	1
E	5	1	F	6	3	C	9	D	2	B	7	8	4	A	G
3	7	B	D	4	2	G	A	1	8	F	5	E	6	C	9
6	A	2	G	5	F	1	8	E	C	4	9	7	B	D	3
F	1	5	8	C	4	9	E	3	B	7	D	6	G	2	A
4	9	C	3	2	7	D	B	8	6	G	A	F	5	1	E
B	D	7	E	G	6	A	3	2	F	5	1	4	C	9	8

Challenge 97

8	4	F	B	G	7	D	2	3	E	A	6	1	5	C	9
C	5	1	9	F	8	4	B	G	2	7	D	6	E	3	A
G	D	7	2	E	6	A	3	1	9	C	5	4	8	F	B
3	6	E	A	1	5	C	9	4	B	F	8	G	7	D	2
9	C	5	1	4	F	B	A	D	7	2	G	E	3	8	6
2	7	G	D	6	E	3	8	C	5	9	1	F	B	A	4
B	F	8	4	7	1	2	D	6	A	E	3	5	C	9	G
A	E	3	6	5	G	9	C	8	F	B	4	7	D	2	1
D	G	2	7	A	3	6	E	9	1	5	C	8	4	B	F
6	8	A	5	9	C	1	F	B	D	4	7	3	2	G	E
1	9	C	E	B	4	8	5	2	3	G	F	D	A	6	7
4	3	B	F	2	D	G	7	A	8	6	E	C	9	1	5
5	1	9	C	8	B	F	4	7	G	D	2	A	6	E	3
F	2	4	G	D	A	7	6	E	C	3	9	B	1	5	8
7	B	D	8	3	2	E	G	5	6	1	A	9	F	4	C
E	A	6	3	C	9	5	1	F	4	8	B	2	G	7	D

Challenge 98

8	E	2	4	3	A	5	7	6	B	1	D	C	9	F	G
9	3	5	G	C	D	1	6	F	E	8	7	2	A	B	4
A	C	7	B	F	2	8	G	5	3	9	4	E	6	1	D
1	F	6	D	E	B	9	4	2	C	A	G	3	8	5	7
5	7	E	A	G	F	B	8	C	D	2	9	4	1	6	3
B	4	3	8	2	C	7	9	G	F	6	1	D	5	E	A
2	D	9	C	4	3	6	1	E	7	5	A	G	F	8	B
6	G	F	1	D	5	E	A	3	4	B	8	7	2	C	9
4	B	A	E	5	9	G	C	1	6	7	3	8	D	2	F
G	5	C	3	B	4	2	E	8	A	D	F	6	7	9	1
D	6	8	9	7	1	A	F	B	2	G	E	5	4	3	C
7	2	1	F	6	8	D	3	9	5	4	C	B	G	A	E
E	A	4	5	8	7	C	B	D	9	F	6	1	3	G	2
3	8	B	7	9	G	4	2	A	1	E	5	F	C	D	6
F	9	D	6	1	E	3	5	4	G	C	2	A	B	7	8
C	1	G	2	A	6	F	D	7	8	3	B	9	E	4	5

Challenge 99

8	C	4	G	D	5	A	1	B	9	E	2	F	7	3	6
9	5	D	1	3	6	8	F	C	7	4	G	2	A	E	B
6	3	A	F	E	B	2	7	8	5	1	D	9	G	4	C
7	B	E	2	4	C	9	G	6	A	3	F	D	5	1	8
C	9	G	4	F	A	6	3	5	8	D	1	7	E	B	2
5	8	1	D	G	9	C	4	7	B	2	E	6	3	F	A
A	F	6	3	7	E	B	2	9	C	G	4	1	8	D	5
B	7	2	E	1	8	5	D	A	6	F	3	C	4	G	9
4	G	C	9	B	2	7	E	F	3	6	A	8	D	5	1
D	1	5	8	C	G	4	9	E	2	7	B	3	6	A	F
3	A	F	6	5	1	D	8	4	G	9	C	B	2	7	E
E	2	B	7	6	F	3	A	1	D	5	8	G	C	9	4
G	4	9	C	8	D	1	5	2	E	B	7	A	F	6	3
1	D	8	5	2	7	E	B	3	F	A	6	4	9	C	G
F	6	3	A	9	4	G	C	D	1	8	5	E	B	2	7
2	E	7	B	A	3	F	6	G	4	C	9	5	1	8	D

Challenge 100

G	3	7	B	E	4	A	6	F	C	5	1	8	9	2	D
F	1	4	C	2	5	8	9	D	A	G	3	B	6	E	7
6	E	5	A	3	D	B	F	7	8	9	2	C	G	1	4
9	2	D	8	1	7	C	G	4	B	6	E	3	F	A	5
2	4	B	F	D	8	6	1	C	G	E	7	9	3	5	A
3	D	8	5	7	C	9	2	A	F	1	4	G	E	6	B
1	7	C	6	4	A	G	E	B	9	3	5	F	2	D	8
E	G	A	9	5	B	F	3	8	6	2	D	7	1	4	C
D	C	6	2	8	G	1	7	9	E	4	B	A	5	3	F
7	8	G	E	C	9	3	4	5	2	F	A	1	D	B	6
4	A	F	1	B	6	E	5	G	3	D	8	2	7	C	9
5	B	9	3	A	F	2	D	6	1	7	C	E	4	8	G
A	9	E	7	F	3	4	B	2	D	8	6	5	C	G	1
C	5	1	G	9	E	D	A	3	4	B	F	6	8	7	2
B	F	3	D	6	2	5	8	1	7	C	G	4	A	9	E
8	6	2	4	G	1	7	C	E	5	A	9	D	B	F	3

ALSO AVAILABLE

Bible Word Searches

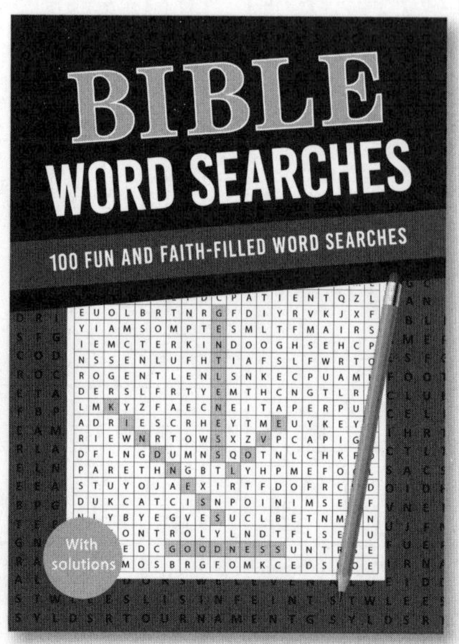

978-0-638-00035-1

Featuring 100 fun and fascinating word searches that range from easy to tricky and cover biblical topics from Genesis to Revelation.

Are you looking for a relaxing activity for quiet evenings at home? Or do you want to spend some quality screen-free time with the kids? Then look no further than ***Bible Word Searches***.

There is sure to be something for everyone with 100 fun and fascinating word searches that range from easy to tricky and cover biblical topics from Genesis to Revelation. You will not only relax and unwind as you search for the words but also discover some interesting facts about Bible times, places and people.

Each word search has a Scripture verse to reflect on and as an added bonus trivia questions have been scattered throughout for an extra challenge. Solutions to each puzzle are provided at the back of the book.